Taking the Work Out of Networking

"Karen Wickre may be the best-connected Silicon Valley figure you've never heard of, widely regarded in tech as a champion networker. Now she reveals in highly readable, practical terms how anyone can create and sustain a network painlessly, and why it matters. This book can change your career, and your life."

—Walt Mossberg, former columnist and
conference producer for the *Wall Street Journal*,
AllThingsDigital, and *Recode*

"Karen Wickre has taken a lifetime of learning and put it into a practical, easy-to-use book that people of all stripes and backgrounds will find useful. (And by the way: it's not only for introverts!)"

—Sree Sreenivasan, former Chief Digital Officer
of New York City, Columbia University, and the
Metropolitan Museum of Art

"Listen to Karen Wickre. *Taking the Work Out of Networking* will make you a better questioner, observer, relationship-nurturer, and, yes—networker for all the right reasons."

—Blair Shane, Chief Marketing Officer,
Sequoia Capital

"If you believe relationships are the bedrock of both adventure and achievement, then you must read this book. Step by step, concept by concept, Karen shares her wisdom on how to build a community of relationships that help you change the world."

—Keith Yamashita, founder and chairman,
SYPartners

"Networking is essential for business success, yet many still dread it. Prepare to change your mind. Karen Wickre's inspired new book shows readers how to embrace their true selves while building an authentic, sustainable network."

—Dorie Clark, adjunct professor at Duke University's Fuqua School of Business and author, *Stand Out Networking* and *Reinventing You*

"Most of us dread the awkward phone calls to strangers and the transactional nature of what we think of as 'networking.' Karen Wickre recasts the notion completely—and extremely usefully—in terms of connections, friendships, and reciprocity. A very user-friendly tool for those of us introverts masquerading as extroverts."

—Amanda Bennett, journalist and author

"For introverts who panic at the idea of networking, Wickre's book is a deep, calming breath. You can do it."

—Sophia Dembling, author of *The Introvert's Way* and *Introverts in Love*

"People will always be moving and changing jobs, but the value of human connection doesn't change. Karen Wickre shows how 'loose-touch' interactions can make your life better. If you're an introvert, you will find help making connections in ways that don't feel forced or artificial. If you know an introvert, this book makes a good gift."

—Matt Cutts, former Googler

TAKING THE WORK OUT OF NETWORKING

An Introvert's Guide to
Making Connections That Count

KAREN WICKRE

TOUCHSTONE
New York   London   Toronto   Sydney   New Delhi

Touchstone
An Imprint of Simon & Schuster, Inc.
1230 Avenue of the Americas
New York, NY 10020

First Touchstone hardcover edition November 2018

TOUCHSTONE and colophon are registered trademarks
of Simon & Schuster, Inc.

For information about special discounts for bulk purchases,
please contact Simon & Schuster Special Sales at 1-866-506-1949
or business@simonandschuster.com.

The Simon & Schuster Speakers Bureau can bring authors to
your live event. For more information or to book an event contact
the Simon & Schuster Speakers Bureau at 866-248-3049
or visit our website at www.simonspeakers.com.

Interior design by Kyle Kabel

Manufactured in the United States of America

10 9 8 7 6 5 4 3 2 1

Library of Congress Cataloging-in-Publication Data is available.

ISBN 978-1-5011-9927-1
ISBN 978-1-5011-9929-5 (ebook)

For Tom, who taught me about fearlessness,
and for all of you who are my tribe. You keep me going.

Collecting the dots. Then connecting them. And then sharing the connections with those around you. This is how a creative human works. Collecting, connecting, sharing.

—*Amanda Palmer*

Contents

Contents

Introduction

Networking is more about farming than it is about hunting.

—*Ivan Misner*

Networking is one of those things most of us think of as a chore—an unloved task to undertake when we need something: a new job, better career guidance, more education, or other useful information. As I was developing the idea of this book, virtually every person I mentioned it to said the same thing: "I hate networking. Anything to help me avoid it, or survive it, would be great." When I asked friends on Twitter and Facebook what specifically they hate about having to network, the replies flew in:

"Everyone's trying to be something they're not."

"The goal-driven artificiality of it. Conversations had for the sake of achieving a goal, rather than for creating connection, feel fake."

"I hate having to have surface-level conversations with people who I will probably forget for the sole mutual purpose of trying to take advantage of the relationship for personal benefit."

As a lifelong introvert, the idea of forcing an introduction, talking too much about myself, or even asking for a business card has always been anathema. I get anxious if my calendar gets crowded with meetings, calls, and other obligations requiring me to talk too much or be in a crowd.

And yet, despite my own need for self-protection and solitude, I've ended up at age sixty-seven with a few thousand contacts across the world. I would never work a room, but I'm not afraid to initiate a conversation with virtually anyone. Over my long and varied career, my network of contacts has come to enrich my life every day. Friends and acquaintances (and the people they know, and so on) regularly come to me for ideas, support, connection, and introductions. And I do the same.

Wherever you fall on the introvert > extrovert spectrum, the *need* to network in order to develop new connections has never mattered more. A few proof points:

- **We change jobs a lot.** Younger baby boomers hold *nearly a dozen different jobs* during their working years, and millennials are projected to hold even more (Bureau of Labor Statistics).
- **Job hopping starts young.** New college grads today *work at twice as many companies* in their first five post-grad years than in earlier eras (LinkedIn).
- **We move a lot.** People in the United States move *more than eleven times* in their lives (FiveThirtyEight.com).
- **More of us work for ourselves.** There are nearly 41 million self-employed Americans aged twenty-one and up, and the trend is growing (MBO Partners, Nation1099.com).

For all of these reasons—job changes, freelance work, geographical moves—it's become incumbent on most all of us to make networking a regular practice. And as we move through our professional lives, we're going to continue to need an ever-changing, ever-growing variety of people to call on. A contemporary definition of "networking" is *to make an effort to meet and talk to a lot of people, especially in order to get information that can help you.* That doesn't sound too bad, right?

Nevertheless, People Hate Having to Do It

But to lots of people, networking conjures up images of pressing a business card on everyone in sight as you make sure to collect an equal number. Other dreaded aspects of networking: having to meet strangers to get in line for a new job; needing the inside scoop on a new field or city; trying to game the hiring system to match your experience to an interesting role. It all seems phony, and baldly transactional. Plus, for all the time we spend avoiding networking, we think we have to get out there exactly when we feel most needy. When things seem at their worst (an impending layoff, dead-end role, intolerable work environment), we feel vulnerable—sometimes even desperate. Who could be their best under these circumstances?

Of course, there are also people who don't believe they need to network. After all, they say, their job is secure. (Until it isn't.) And there are some who feel resigned to their current job because, frankly, they can't imagine anything better, or feel they can't afford, for any number of reasons (tenure, title downgrade, lower compensation, commuting logistics, and so on), to make a switch. A friend described to me the lifelong conundrum of networking: "Traditionally one is raised to not discuss work in social situations, to not be self-important, not be self-promoting, not be opportunistic, not make use of one's friends—and then, as a professional adult, one has to somehow integrate the need to market oneself. The conflict never seems to feel any less awkward."

For introverts, multiply that distaste and even fear about having to connect with strangers. No less a figure than Carl Jung has described an introvert as someone who needs solo time to recharge, who regains energy by spending time alone—whereas extroverts get a special charge by being in a crowd and having lots of human contact without seeming to need a break. Most of us are somewhere along the spectrum between the two. In my own experience, and from what I've heard from kindred spirits, we who tilt toward introversion are more at home with our thoughts than we are in a chattering crowd. The idea of having to elbow our way into a conversation or a noisy room is just about the worst chore imaginable. Before I head back out in the world, I need unscheduled time for my brain to wander and rejuvenate. You, too?

All of the negatives associated with networking can lead to some mighty magical thinking when we face a big job or career change, or even simply recognize the need to make a change. The fantasy is that we will hear directly about the perfect new role; our resume will make it to the top of the pile; our friend on the inside will help us cinch it. Or maybe the magical thinking is: we're fine where we are, and there's no need to do anything for a long time to come, if ever (because it's too horrible to consider networking). Like I say, it's magic!

My Long and Nonstrategic Trip

The fact, though, is that for many of us, making career and life moves is more a mix of fits and starts than it is a grand plan or a seamless upward trajectory. I offer myself as Exhibit #1, with as long and unplanned a career in Silicon Valley as one could have. By today's standards, my career in tech began late: I was thirty-five in the mid-1980s when I got into the then-lively world of personal computer magazines. My longtime passion for writing and editing helped me to become a consumer tech journalist, a (reluctant) PR flack, and an editorial and project manager for startups and creative agencies. Not a straight path, in other words.

In 2000, Silicon Valley experienced a major economic downturn. I had joined an eighteen-person startup that year, an early e-commerce personal gift business called Violet.com. Four tumultuous months later, we turned off the lights for good; no second round of funding was forthcoming. I went on to an established creative agency that was opening a San Francisco office. That turned out to be bad timing (downturns don't lead to clients), and before long the firm decamped to its LA office—without me. By the end of the year, there were very few jobs to pursue, and not much contract work. No one was hiring. Over the next fifteen months or so I struggled with not enough work or money. I started an informal support group for a few friends in the same boat. We met weekly to cheer each other on and share leads. I reached out to lots of contacts to see if they might need writing help. One of these calls was to a friend I'd worked with twice before, who had recently taken a job at a startup called Google. I asked if she needed any writing help; she told me they just hired a marketing writer but promised to keep me in mind.

A couple of months later, she called back. It seemed work was piling up. Would I come in and meet the team? She stressed that she couldn't hire me directly; others would have to like my work (and me). I must have been a port in a storm, because at that very first meeting they asked me to jump in, which I did eagerly, working from home. Within a couple of weeks, it was clear that I should spend more time in the office to get face time with the team. I began the daily seventy-mile-round-trip commute to Google HQ. Once I became a regular fixture, I raised my hand for every assignment. I wanted to be seen as indispensable as possible, because I could see Google was somewhere I'd like to be. Not a big partier by nature, I even hosted cocktail gatherings at my flat for the team—the team I wasn't yet on. My goal was to become as familiar as the bean bag seating around the office so people would know they could rely on me, and that I was suitably Googley. It took fifteen months for all the forces to converge for me to be hired into a full-time role as senior editor (a title I made up, by the way). I then remained at Google for eight more wonderful and life-changing years.

I recite this history for two reasons. One, I was able to call on someone in my network to make a meaningful connection when I really needed it. (It's worth noting, too, that my friend was someone with whom I had stayed in loose touch, a habit I discuss in chapter 3.) Two, once I got a toehold inside Google, my work output was just the start: networking *inside* the organization was critical, especially as it grew very quickly from hundreds to thousands of employees. I had to rely on my soft skills—communication, empathy, curiosity—to maintain credibility with both men and women, technical and not, virtually all of whom were younger than me.

Today I see both of these moves as hallmarks of my style of organic networking. I say "organic" because it's instinctive: *I do it when I don't need anything.* One result is that I have a casual and friendly acquaintance with lots of people, because I use these soft skills as a matter of course. Friends sometimes say that I "know everyone." That's not true, of course—but I do have a good sense of *who everyone is.* In other words, I remember names and connections; I keep up with people's accomplishments and job changes. That turns out to matter for networking. It's a mark of curiosity about who else is out in the world, who's making news, who's interesting, who's connected to people I already know. To me, such knowledge is a key part of the introvert's observational powers.

It surprises people when I tell them I think it's precisely because of my introverted nature that I've cultivated a kind of personal strength that comes from access to wide-ranging connections.

The Tools You Already Have

It may seem ironic, but I think we introverts have qualities that make us very effective networkers. One example: our interest in others exceeds our need to talk about ourselves. When I meet someone, I'm much more comfortable asking, "What's new with you?" or "Tell me about yourself." This move gives me time to size up the person. A psychologist might say people enjoy my company because I let them have the floor. It is true that even as an introvert, I want to be liked (a default setting, apparently, for girls born in the 1950s). Whatever the reason, I always begin encounters anywhere but with me.

Another essential for networking is being a good observer—a clear advantage we have over chattier peers. I am forever wondering about who people are and why they are that way. What's their demeanor, what's their history, what animates or irritates them? I observe, and somehow, I remember and apply that knowledge as needed.

An equally vital and underleveraged element in the introvert's arsenal is the use of social media and digital communication to reach people in ways that may feel more natural. By making good use of online interactions, it's frankly easier to connect with people both within and outside your company minus the dread of working the room. This book will show you how participating in social media services, even lightly, gives introverts an advantage when it comes to staying in loose touch—an essential daily habit that helps us feel connected and empowered from the safe distance of our screens.

This book is about how to create and nurture your own wide-ranging, authentic network for life. I'll show you how to approach the making and following up of meaningful connections; how to call on others you don't know well for advice and favors, how to give as much, or more, as you get, and how all of this can help you feel more fulfilled and secure—all while remaining true to your natural self.

I'm going to do my best in this book to encourage you to approach networking with a sense of curiosity and open-mindedness that will help you cultivate meaningful connections with many people as your needs and interests evolve, without the obligation of constant contact. When you can do this and not fret about it, you, too, can build or grow your own brain trust: a web of connections to call on for ideas, opportunities, and experiences you might have missed otherwise.

Whether you're shy or self-effacing, heading to a new city or new line of work, or even too busy to focus on any of this—I hope to offer a different way to think about how you make, and keep, meaningful professional and personal connections that can be yours for life. To make all of this less of an onerous task and more of a natural, and even welcome, part of your day. With luck, this book will help you channel your natural instincts to build your network in a way that's true to your nature.

Now then—let's get going.

PART ONE

THE ELEMENTS
OF CONNECTING

When, out of the fear of the unknown, we shut
ourselves off from links to one another, we lose as
individuals, as companies, and as institutions. When
we open up, we gain new chances to learn, connect,
and collaborate.

—Jeff Jarvis

Unleashing the Introvert's Secret Power

> The secret to life is to put yourself in the right light-
> ing. For some, it's a Broadway spotlight; for others,
> a lamplit desk.
>
> —*Susan Cain*

The notion of networking as needing to be "on"—to shake every hand and capture every soul (for a minute, anyway)—is something we tend to think extroverts do well, and introverts—not so much. But when it comes to making connections, introverts may have the upper hand. You don't have to change who you are or concoct a phony-feeling persona to meet people easily.

Let's take a moment to review what "introvert" really means. In the 1920s, Swiss psychologist Carl Jung developed his theory of psychological types, noting that "Each person seems to be energized more by either the external world (*extraversion*) or the internal world (*introversion*)." Much more recently, the *Urban Dictionary* built on that idea: "Contrary to popular belief, not all introverts are shy. Some may have great social lives and love talking to their friends but just need some time to be alone to 'recharge' afterwards."

That part about recharging is key. As Jung observed, extroverts typically gain energy from being in a crowd—a party, a game, concert, hopping from one gathering to another. Those of us at the other end of the spectrum need quiet time to regroup, think, plan, and dream. I'm not alone, I'm sure, in mentally calculating how long it will be till I can get *away* from the crowd. No matter how lovely a time I'm having at a group event, I always look forward to being back home.

Another mark of the introvert is the ability to be comfortable being quiet, which is often misunderstood. As a thoughtful and introspective teenager, my goal was to observe and eavesdrop on adult conversations. When my parents had guests over, I was intrigued by the *sotto voce* remarks they would make later, speculating about the (unspoken) troubles they knew their friends were having. Nothing had been uttered at the table, of course, which led me to understand that human experiences run much deeper than polite company revealed. I began to feel like an anthropologist—the outsider studying the group with a cool eye, never fully joining in.

I'm convinced that all of these qualities, which introverts seem to share—feeling like an outsider, being an observer, curiosity about the stories and situations of others—inform how I've made my way through life. (As one scholarly study put it, "An introvert who is silent in a group may actually be quite engaged—taking in what is said, thinking about it, waiting for a turn to speak.") I think this ability to observe and assess are some of my best assets, and maybe they're yours, too. Whether you're shy, humble, self-effacing, insecure, or simply hate the stereotype of networking, I want to encourage you to make the most of your own personal style in order to build your own brain trust—to start from where you are.

My long-held theory is that introverts (and other unassuming people) are well suited to building a strong web of connections because of some distinctive characteristics we share, such as these:

- **We're good at listening.** When I meet someone for the first time, I make a game out of getting them to talk first—to give up more personal information than I give. That may sound cold, but it gives me time to size them up, to assess my ability to trust them. If I get a good feeling, then I'll open up (a little). This is a key tactic: *ask questions first.* You learn to sort out how much you want to invest in another person when they're talking to (or at) you. It's much more important to use your listening skills than to jump in to talk. And once you've listened, you will have options about where or how far to go in what you say.

- **We're keen observers.** Even though feeling like an outsider might seem isolating, the fact that you don't take up all the social space (as some of our extrovert friends can do) lets others reveal who they are as you take it all in. I have a lifelong habit of observing people—what can I deduce about them from a personal meeting or from sitting across from them on the subway? Who seems excitable, self-assured, angry, depressed—and why? When I meet someone, I tend to remember a few distinctive things about them—their interests, hometown, personal style, alma mater—that help me approach people right where they are. And this skill is so beneficial to connecting with someone else. You put yourself into the mind-set of another, which puts them at ease and helps you forge a meaningful encounter.

- **We're curious.** When you feel like an outsider, you assume others have mastered life—connecting with people, navigating choices, pursuing a path—in ways you have not. Keen observers tend to put those observations to work. As a quiet kid, I was always curious about how other people navigated the world, and especially how they seemed to fit in, where I didn't feel like I did. (A blessing, of sorts, about adulthood: you learn that very few people actually feel like they fit right.)

These abilities—listening, observing, being curious—are wonderful tools for connecting with people. And here's the thing: *none of them requires you to be in the limelight.* That doesn't mean you can't have a successful career, of course.

For more than twenty years, Judy Wert has led her own executive recruiting firm in New York for companies in search of creative leadership. If you think a search consultant must be super-outgoing to succeed, meet Judy, who considers herself an introvert. She thinks of herself as a kind of "gentle provocateur" who plays a long game, professionally, out of necessity. Headhunters and recruiters must always meet new people to keep in mind for future client needs. She's intentionally kept her firm small to employ a high-touch approach driven by her relationships across her global network.

A visual designer, Judy morphed her design tools into a new "medium of people," which has made Wert&Co. "the story of people and conversations." She has tracked these ongoing conversations through her proprietary custom-designed database—built long before LinkedIn or Salesforce—which is a repository for the thousands of people she's met. It's not unusual for her to follow up years later about an opportunity with an individual she met only once.

When I think of Judy, I think of someone whose work revolves around the qualities I've mentioned here: curiosity, observation, listening. She describes her process of matching people to positions as one of "strategic intuition"—a sensibility that captures the kind of calibration, internal and external, that introverts know very well. I admit to some bias here: I think introverts are more attuned to the steady thrum of needs, desires, secrets, and worries most people experience. That awareness informs our understanding of others, for the better.

It's this notion that helps us think more roundly (and smartly) about who would be the right one for an open position, and more broadly, the right person to critique your resume; to be the executor of your will; the right friend with whom to enjoy the latest action movie or dive bar; the best brainstormer to develop your food truck idea—and a thousand other things. You already have a sense of who'd you want for some of these things, through the recommendations of friends or previous experiences. The same skill works when you apply it to a wider array of contacts that can help you with many of the choices there are to make throughout your career, and indeed throughout life.

Listening, observing, being curious—all are wonderful tools for connecting with people. And here's the thing: none of them requires you to be in the limelight.

The combination of introversion and observation provides a great gift: the art of sizing people up. We can sense the makeup of someone pretty quickly: are they needy, clueless, boastful, nervous? Do they evoke equilibrium, curiosity, good humor? Sensing such qualities means that you have a good grip on what to ask or expect of anyone you meet—and that's a handy skill as you continue to build your network.

TRY IT OUT: Exercise Your Introvert Powers

Here are three exercises to warm you up to the idea of using your abilities to help grow your web of connections. Give them a try! I think you'll find that people will feel good as a result of your effort, and you'll learn things you can draw on later with them or others.

Ask questions first.

Next time you're having coffee with someone you don't know well (or at all—a coworker, friend of friend, fellow conference-goer), prompt them to tell you their story first. This works well by phone, too.

Your opening line can be as simple as:

"We'll get to me, but first I would love to hear how you [like working at company X] or [have made your mark in X field or specialty or accomplishment]. "

or

"I'm still thinking about that conference/speaker. What has stayed with you from that talk?"

Especially if you are trying to find work in their company or industry, follow that with an invitation that's a question:

"How did you get into company X?"

"How long have you held job Y?"

"Do you enjoy profession Z?"

Put your curiosity to work.

Curiosity is a mental skill, something you activate whether or not you're meeting in person. When you are having an informational meeting (including by phone or video chat) with someone from the company or field you're interested in, do your homework to make the best use of their time and yours by jumping right to the heart of what you're there to do. After initial pleasantries, for example, tailor your opening gambit to the kind of topic you're pursuing:

"What I want to know is, how did you get the cat out of the chimney?!" (Referencing what you saw on their Instagram feed; an icebreaker that shows you're paying attention to what they're about.)

"What was it like to be at Google in the early years?" (You learned this from LinkedIn.)

"Do you enjoy writing regularly?" (You read their site, newsletter, or blog.)

Be a keen observer.
Where curiosity is largely mental, observation is more physical. It works best in person and has great value when you're meeting someone new. Part of being a keen observer is how well you can put your new contact at ease (more often than guaranteeing a solid connection), and part of it is gathering your own sense of him or her.

Some ways to work observation into the conversation:

"Your glasses are so great—do you collect them?" (*Clothing can be too personal to call out at a first meeting, but glasses or shoes are fairer to compliment.*)

"How do you like your phone cover/battery/notepad/ pen?" (*Which accessories they keep nearby tells you a bit about them.*)

Some things to consider during your conversation:

Are they ill at ease and fidgety, or do they seem relaxed and comfortable?

Are they strictly business, or do they reveal a bit about themselves, their preferences, or quirks?

Your observational powers are also very helpful in group meetings:

Ever notice the one person who is always the naysayer, or the interrupter?

The "meeting after the meeting" person who can only debrief later?

Who always has time for a friendly personal word, and who doesn't?

What you observe gives you an extra sense of understanding of others, and that can make your connections work more smoothly—simply based on who they show you they are.

Why Networking Matters

*There is simply too much to be gained from working
in tandem with the rest of the world.*

—*David Benson*

As I mention in the introduction, Americans change jobs frequently. We tend to move locations a lot over our lifetimes, and most of those moves occur after age thirty. And then there's the rise of self-employment, as well as what some call "micro-employment," or the gig economy—which means piecing together several jobs in order to have more money, time, or both. In a prescient 2007 essay, writer and entrepreneur Penelope Trunk suggests that staying in one job for three years is a good practice: "If you change jobs frequently, you build an adaptable skill set and a wide network which are the keys to being able to find a job whenever you need to."

With our habits of moving around and changing jobs becoming ingrained, you can see why it's more important than ever to keep up contact with work colleagues, past employers, and professional acquaintances. The network you build can serve many purposes: as a reality check for whatever ideas you're hatching, as a gateway to new opportunities you might not have considered, as a resource for leads. Your contacts may include personal friends, but you need

19

more than those. You want to count on a richer mix of people that includes those with whom you've worked in the past; professional contacts; conference and workshop acquaintances; recruiters you've met; and a big passel of friendly acquaintances—people you may have followed, or followed you, on Twitter or Instagram, your LinkedIn connections, and the many people you've come across related to work or school. These are your "weak ties," and I write more about them in chapter 4.

Workarounds to Suit You

In traditional "work the room" network building, the idea is to collect a large number of contacts, and a contact database that's overflowing, so you can blast them with your needs and questions. But honestly, there is no law of large numbers governing your own contacts. There's not a magic number you need to have or claim to know. Thoughtful networkers describe the quality of their contacts, not the quantity. My former colleague Hunter Walk, now a venture capitalist in San Francisco, describes himself as an introvert "who gets slightly anxious during prolonged exposure to big groups." In his line of work, Hunter has to meet many people as a matter of course. He measures success in unavoidable group settings (such as conferences) as connecting with as few as five or ten people over a day when he might be with hundreds. In Hunter's world, even a handful of those ten or fifteen people might help him discover promising new companies. His criterion for such connections? What he describes as "meaningful conversations."

Similarly, executive recruiter Judy Wert says she gauges her success in being able to connect people to opportunities though her "learning mindset and curiosity" with clients and candidates alike. She's always looking for the human connections that "inspire great and authentic conversation, which in turn inspires great referrals."

She told me she never thinks of herself as "networking"—a word that doesn't resonate with her. Instead, she says, "I am simply a connector of people."

TRY IT OUT: Make a Meaningful Connection

If you're attuned to these three elements, you can make a good contact in as little as twenty or thirty minutes. And remember, a good contact—a meaningful connection—is not measured in numbers. As Ivan Misner, the founder of BNI (Business Network International) has said, "If your network is a mile wide and an inch deep, it will never be successful." Here are three ways to help you start making deeper connections:

Find common ground quickly.
This can be the person who's introduced you, the fact that you're attending the same event, or are in the same field. It's whatever common ground you have, however slight, that lets you begin the conversation.

Opener: "Alicia and I worked together two jobs ago. How do you know her?"

Share a story.
Each of you having a turn to tell the other one something about yourself creates a bond. It can be as basic as how you landed your job or why you live where you live. Reveal a bit of personality instead of simply reciting the bare bones. What you feel like revealing is a measure of whether your bond is growing.

Opener: "I was an army brat, and that's what led me to real estate. I want to help people put down roots."

Discover a future to-do.

If in the course of your conversation you learn that you're both taking an upcoming class, starting a blog, going to a reception or conference next month, or anything similar, you've found a kindred spirit. If the conversation leads to more formal contact or collaboration in the near future, even better.

Opener: "I'm really looking forward to your presentation on user research next month. If you need to practice running through your deck, I'd be happy to help."

Note that both Hunter and Judy stress the quality of connections you make. One of the best ways to do that is to avoid thinking of each encounter as a transaction. If you treat your contacts as a kind of personal ATM for frequent withdrawals, you'll quickly be disappointed, not to mention overdrawn. No one likes to feel used repeatedly, especially when it's one-sided. (And you don't like being treated that way either. Right?) The best connections you can make are those where you have mutuality: sometimes one of you needs something, and sometimes neither of you does, and you continue to give your time and attention either way.

> If you treat your connections as a kind of personal ATM you use for frequent withdrawals, you'll quickly be disappointed (and overdrawn).

By the way, there's no expiration date on you or your connections helping each other. People I haven't worked with (or even laid eyes on) for years pop up on occasion to schedule a meeting or call to kick around ideas and contacts; I do the same. In our world of frequent job changes and moves, it's not at all unusual to lose direct contact after one of you has moved on. But if you have made meaningful connections, that's fine. Even over the course of writing this book, I've reached out to people I haven't worked with for twenty years. Our connection continues.

In the next chapter, I'll talk about what I call "loose touch"—the care and feeding of your networks over time—which I consider the gold standard for nurturing your network. Before we move on, though, let me lay down a few guidelines that can make for the most fruitful and personally satisfying network—for your immediate needs, as well as for the long haul. These guidelines apply whether you need help, or you are the one helping. The fact is that all of us will be on both sides of this equation from time to time.

---

11 Organizing Principles of No-Pressure Networking

1. **Be open.** Pick your favorite: both Robert De Niro and Smash Mouth are credited with saying, "If you don't go, you'll never know"—that's the essence here. Believe that the odds favor an encounter or exchange, however brief, that will be interesting, enlightening—and worth those moments of connection. More practically speaking, we all have times when we need to figure out a next step; clarify priorities; get a sense of the job, city, health, school, and so on. *No single source will be enough,* so it's imperative to be open to people. Sometimes the payoff is in learning that you really *don't* want to work for that company or move to another city. But you'll only learn that when you're open to meeting and asking.

2. **"Just because" is reason enough.** How do you start making new connections? I'm a big believer in the brief coffee date,

even if you don't know what the value, or even the agenda, might be. Sometimes the reason to meet is that someone said to each of us, "I know you two will like each other." Among my recent coffee dates have been a startup guy who wanted to brainstorm with a variety of people about his idea; PR pros wanting to jump from tech to consumer services, or vice versa; a veteran journalist one step ahead of a pink slip at a collapsing publication. (A sad fact of the media world today.) Virtually all of these meetups have led to delightful conversations with ideas sparking on both sides, and the start of a beautiful connection. You just don't know where such casual and perhaps agenda-less meetings might go.

3. **Be helpful.** On the theory that what goes around comes around, and that in fact we need to rely on others throughout our lives, your default setting should be "I want to help, even if I don't know how." Our work and social worlds have gotten too small to keep doors shut (or risk being seen as an unhelpful jerk). When someone reaches out—even to say "I need a new job, but I don't know what I want" to you, offer to chat. Not every idea or introduction is worth a lot of time, but even if you can't help much (or aren't inclined to), be polite about it. A simple "Sorry, but I don't know anyone in defense contracting—good luck!" is better than silence. When people ask me for some kind of help, I don't want them to go away empty-handed. Even those mildly annoying notes from people I don't know on LinkedIn asking me to help them get verified on Twitter—something I can't do—lead me to send a Twitter support link on that topic, and wish them luck. In short: Don't get all quid pro quo about it—just pay it forward and help out.

4. **Play a long game.** Of course, making meaningful connections is itself a long game—a cumulative process. And a long game requires patience! That initial introduction or meeting may lead

nowhere. The same is true when someone seeks my advice. We get acquainted a bit, and then the brainstorming begins. It's rare that I'll know precisely the right person for somebody's initial request—say, the hiring manager for a specific, and current, job listing. Most of the time, your friend or contact won't have that direct link either. And sometimes the request is more about brainstorming: ideas for a workshop facilitator, the right speaker or panelist for a conference, a policy or legal expert for a particular issue. Many times, names do come to mind—that is, people who might know something about something. This is how a network unfolds: you suggest, they suggest, followed by outreach to yet more people after the meeting. As I see it, my job as a connector is to offer whatever context and ideas I can and think broadly about interesting and relevant people who may know more, who may lead to answers.

5. **Don't limit your context.** This is the biggest obstacle I see people impose on themselves: a very limited, and narrow, notion about who or what is going to be useful for their immediate need. *Only* the hiring manager or the principal will do, they think—not the adjacent people who may well have important perspectives, history, broader knowledge, or other good leads. *Don't talk yourself out of the help you need.* This is why I'm careful with introductions. If someone asking for ideas and contacts politely rejects who I'm suggesting because they don't see the logic, I'm not likely to offer again.

6. **Make good referrals.** Just as you would want someone to refer you to a job perfectly suited to you, you want the referrals *you* give to be valuable. In fact, this is one way to become known as a good connector. When someone asks for your ideas, it matters to understand the context—industry, strategy, audience—for which they need leads. Now and then I ask to meet with people at service businesses (in my world these are

often design, marketing, PR, or strategy firms) to hear about what they offer. I do this so I can have referral suggestions on hand when someone asks me for leads. In your travels, it pays to be curious and learn about what other people do so you can build a mental file of jobs, businesses and fields. Knowing a major multinational event producer is great if someone you know needs a rock-concert-style show, but not so much when someone at a ten-person startup needs guidance on designing their first trade show booth. So, too, introducing your freelance journalist friend to your neighbor wanting corporate sales copy probably won't lead to a happy ending. Take in all information about the specifics, and use your judgment to make good calls. Don't make random or bad suggestions just to fulfill a request!

7. **Keep your word.** Here's the part you cannot overlook, and the very point of having a network: the follow-up. If you proffer leads, *you have to follow through* to make introductions or forward the request. Don't toy with people who have asked for your help! If you're asked to have a conversation that requires scheduling, don't jam yourself up and risk flaking out; it's fine to set a time to talk by phone or meet in person a few weeks out. And if you truly can't help—you don't have time, good ideas, or applicable contacts—just say so, kindly and quickly. Don't leave the request dangling because you think you'll come back to it later (you probably won't). Believe me: when it's your turn, you will want the same aboveboard treatment.

8. **Make introductions correctly.** When you have ideas for who should meet whom, write to your personal contact and ask if they mind an introduction. Here are the steps involved, and the variables you need to adjust for:

   • First, send a note to your contact explaining what the question or need is, and ask if they're willing to talk with your contact. Explain how you know the person, why you are

helping, and how you think your contact can help specifically.

- *Only when they say yes do you move ahead to introductions.*
  With an okay in hand, write to both parties, briefly recapping
  the common ground or the query, and sign off.

- *Pro tip:* move the connector to bcc: in email (or, if you're
  the connector, remind the others to drop you off the rest
  of the exchange; I'm amazed at how often I'm still included
  as they sort out the logistics of scheduling).

- Occasionally in this scenario my contact doesn't follow up,
  and I will nudge them ever so gently—once—to see if they've
  forgotten to reply. Sometimes even that's a dead end, but
  usually the nudgee is grateful for the reminder.

- Also, never make a cold introduction with both parties
  included on that first message without an okay from the
  one you're asking for a favor. I readily agree to most requests
  when my contact asks me first if it's all right to proceed; I'm
  almost always irritated when the combo intro appears out of
  nowhere, with no context. Some people use the shorthand
  "double opt-in" for this process.

9. **Don't under-communicate.** Again and again people tell me
   they're reluctant to get in touch, follow up, or ask a favor when
   they have an unanswered question or an unsolved problem.
   Given the ubiquity of email (call me old-fashioned, but it's still
   the best way to keep in touch with a vast swath of people you
   don't know well), it could not be easier or more efficient to ping
   people and ask, clarify, follow up, or quickly learn something.
   And when you're on the hunt for real—when you are formally
   pursuing a job—you *have* to be more communicative than
   usual. When you're actively seeking a specific job, company,
   or introduction, be sure to thank your contacts (regardless of
   what they did) along the way and inform them as your process

unfolds. As she followed up with each referral I had given her, I was delighted to get a thank-you from a young woman I met during her job quest. Each one was a brief update (note: being communicative doesn't mean being long-winded!) on the state of her search and how she enjoyed her meetings. She's a great networker, and I'd happily help her again.

And, of course, if the contacts you've made are the exact reason you got what you wanted, go all out with the thank-yous. A former coworker recently asked me to be a reference as she pursued two job openings simultaneously. I was happy to take both recruiters' calls and sang her praises to each. She let me know her thoughts about considering both roles, and then when she accepted one, she sent me a gift—and I'm sure she did that for each person she'd asked to help. It's never a bad idea to express your gratitude and appreciation.

10. **Make real-world 1:1 connections.** All of this might strike you as a lot of work. Can't you just post on Facebook, or tweet, or query LinkedIn or Quora and be done with it? Each of these platforms certainly has a place for finding and trading information and connections, as we'll get into in chapter 6. But don't limit yourself to those, where you will get random and self-selected responses, none as detailed, nuanced, or private as you probably need. And whether it's private or public, these platforms default to our making lazy (if well-intentioned) responses. We've all chimed in with three- or four-word replies to a question posed to a group. Nothing is going to give you the same quality and depth as your personal network can. But honestly, a 1:1 connection that lives over time is going to be much more rewarding than 1:some. Collectively, this is a group you can tap for ideas, referrals, and support. Properly tended, it's yours for life, through all the kinds of obstacles and challenges life brings.

11. **Make a list.** Check it twice. Pause your regular routine every week or so to reflect on what you need answers to or who's asking for your help and ideas. If you organize your email with stars or other priority indicators, go back and follow up on those requests and replies you put off earlier. In the same vein, who haven't you checked in with lately that you'd like to hear from? This is a good time to reach out for a quick "loose-touch" moment, which we'll get to in the next chapter.

Because we live in a world of many unknowns, the more you can learn from others—whether it's for a job opening, medical advice, travel destination, career change, or really getting any kind of foothold—helps you see around corners. The more you can ask for and give help to others, the more knowns emerge—and we're all better off. So, throw off your zero-sum blinders and get going.

The Loose-Touch Habit

Think about how you would approach a potential friend. Find something you have in common, keep it light, make jokes, and above all, show that you care.

—*Sourav Dey*

There are two things in particular people seem to hate about having to network. One is its baldly transactional nature. *Harvard Business Review* offers a wry (and not inaccurate) definition: "the unpleasant task of trading favors with strangers." It seems we humans are put off by such a seemingly blatant purpose. Second, the notion that you might *need* to network feels like a vulnerability. Reaching out to ask someone to put in a good word to a hiring manager, or getting a lead about a new opening, can make you feel desperate (shouldn't you be able to do this on your own?). And having to put yourself in the hands of a stranger, or near stranger, for such help is stressful, too. Add to that any kind of time pressure—say if you've suddenly lost your job, a loan has come due, or you're in the midst of family upheaval—and you're likely to feel abjectly bad about yourself at a time when you need to appear to be on solid footing. That makes it doubly hard to put yourself out there.

Here's a little secret: at some point, every one of us is going to need help from someone we don't currently know. Maybe it's for a job, or family help; it might be about a necessary career pivot, or relocation; it could be for medical or retirement guidance. You—and virtually everyone else—are going to want to reach out to a number of people for contacts, information or insights, or support. And the same is true for others who will have these same needs, who will reach out to you. If remembering this helps you get over thinking of vulnerability as a weakness, that's good! Presumably you're already okay with giving a friendly ear to other people; now it's time to get okay with seeking help for yourself. That's key to making this whole thing work.

Networking When You Don't Need To

Another key to overcoming your fears about networking for a need is to practice a little bit every day—and do it when you *don't* need specific help. I call this "keeping in loose touch": you pop up now and again to your connections, and new acquaintances, too, without any formal obligation to follow up or see one another in person. (It's fine if you do, but loose touch doesn't demand in-person visits very often.) If you do this habitually when you're not feeling needy, you'll begin to see yourself as a giver, not a taker. If you can even occasionally be a problem-solver for others, that helps you get over the fear of feeling needy.

This is my guiding principle for no-pressure networking: *Nurture it before you need it.*

This is my guiding principle for an easier way to network: *Nurture it before you need it.* Today we have more ways than ever to keep in loose touch with people we know or have just met. In chapter 6, there's a lot more information on making the most of your preferred social channels to share, comment, inquire, banter, survey a crowd.

The Beauty of Asynchronicity

Long ago, my own loose-touch habit consisted of a well-worn address book whose cover always had a fresh Post-it list of the phone calls I would make each day. The list represented tasks I needed to do, plus a few people I'd been thinking about. I'd make those calls (or leave messages) and cross them off the list. Whomever I missed would go on the next day's Post-it. Fast forward to the twenty-first century: today, picking up the phone is my *last* resort for keeping in loose touch. Non-voice usage—text, search, email—on mobile phones surpassed voice calls nearly a decade ago, in 2010.

Apart from the explosive growth of mobile phones for everything other than calls, we've become accustomed to many services based on time-shifting—meaning that we can do something when we want to, rather than at a set time. We've become asynchronous, in other words: We no longer have to call a retailer to put in an order or ask about a delivery. We don't have to wait for a store to open or run around looking for a specific item in our desired volume/color/size. We don't watch the six o'clock news; for better or worse, news comes to us 24/7. We've gotten extremely used to working, buying, socializing, and collaborating through many such time shifts.

Communications, too, have time-shifted. Texting, searching, direct messaging, and even old reliable email, are all asynchronous—none requires the immediacy of a phone call. And these are more convenient ways to connect or get answers. You don't have to worry about interrupting anyone, because they can respond when they're free. Asynchronicity is also perfect for introverts, who may shy away from the immediacy of a real-time conversation. You can take the time to compose thoughtful messages, since you're not as on-the-spot for the perfect response.

In an insightful essay, "The Power of Asynchronous Communication," media strategist David Benson observes that when we let go of communicating only in real time in favor of email or other "you'll see it when you see it" messaging, we can "maintain the essential bonds of friendship and dialog" with friends and acquaintances alike.

On Giving and Taking

This may be the crux of connecting with other people: how we approach giving when we don't need to and taking when we do. Networking requires both, and the understanding you bring in the moment to either task. In his book *The Gift*, Lewis Hyde writes with great insight about what he calls the "gift economy" and the value of reciprocity. Instead of limiting ourselves to tit-for-tat exchanges, he writes, it's better to act on the idea that "a gift is kept alive by its constant donation."

The Art of Giving

It's in this spirit that I suggest your networking habit build around what you have to give to others. Twenty years ago, I didn't set out to amass a lot of contacts or cash in on a bunch of favors. What I had was a strong desire for two things: one, make meaningful connections with people, because they helped me feel less alone in the world; and two, share those connections with others for the advice or answers they needed. The simple truth is, I don't like anyone to go away empty-handed. I want to be useful. I don't always have the right information, let alone a perfect solution, but I do have faith that between some number of us, good answers emerge. I want to increase the odds of resolving an open question through my connections. And I like the mutual puzzle-solving that occurs when a couple of us think through the next steps to take, the next contacts to reach out to.

When someone tells me they don't have time to connect in order to help someone, I always think, *What does it cost you to make a little time?* Part of the payoff that awaits is hearing someone's story and making a wonderful connection instead of passing it by. The serendipity of it may be as valuable as anything else. Seattle entrepreneur Julie Schlosser, a "master connector" you'll hear more about later in this chapter, says she thinks connecting and sharing connections is "kind of like donating money. It brings happiness that you can't really explain . . . that's like a religious rule, Ten Commandment–type thing." I feel the same way.

I don't want to suggest you should drop everything in the moment to meet a stranger. We all have obligations and deadlines to deal with. When I agree to meet someone I don't know, usually to hear about their job quest and think of introductions I can make, I'll do it when I have time, which might be weeks away. Email connections are easier and quicker, of course, as they can happen at your convenience. I'm always willing to tap out an email and wait for a reply before I connect two people.

> If you can approach networking based on what *you* can give someone else, it lessens the awkwardness you may feel about what you need.

If you can approach networking based on what *you* can give someone else, it lessens the awkwardness you may feel about what you need. There will be times when you do need new ideas, introductions, guidance—we all do. Until then, there are going to be many chances for you to offer your gifts of listening, brainstorming, and making introductions to others. As I always find myself reminding people, no matter what you do, you have knowledge that can be useful to others. Perhaps Lewis Hyde's opening line in *The Gift* says it best: "What is good is given back."

What You Can Give, What You Can Take

Give

- Praise specifically, not just through likes or hearts
- LinkedIn recommendations to others
- Offer to review presentations or writing

Take

- Receive compliments graciously (don't downplay them)
- Support when it's offered
- Meaningful feedback you can learn from

The Art of Taking

So often when we need advice or introductions, we're hoping for a single touchpoint that will solve our problem. I'm sure I'm not alone in wishing that my favorite search engine (or Magic 8-Ball) would just deliver the right answer: *OK, Google, what's my perfect job? Which field best suits me? Where should I live? Which is the best school to go to, or degree to get?* Wouldn't it be great if we could simply go to the top result for our query and from there apply, join, pay a deposit (or whatever) to get where we want to be? But precious few perfectly formed answers come to us in such a straightforward single step.

Being perennially poised for a wonderful surprise is a great quality. But my practical self, and probably yours, understands that we have to prepare ourselves to ask—to take—along the way, as well as give. Musician Amanda Palmer has explored the idea of taking in her book *The Art of Asking*. As she tells the story, for a long time she was a street performer who scratched together money for recording sessions when she could. Eventually, she launched what became a very successful Kickstarter campaign to get funds to support her work. It was then Palmer realized "often it is our own sense that we are undeserving of help that has immobilized us. Whether it's in the arts, at work, or in our relationships, we often resist asking not only because we're afraid of rejection but also because we don't even think we *deserve* what we're asking for."

If you're thinking, *Okay, but I'm not famous. How does this apply to me?* I'm not suggesting everyone launch an online campaign. The larger point is that Palmer overcame her internal reservations about asking others to support her work. When her fans gave, she was able to take what she had asked for. That was the key to Palmer's new awareness of the dynamic between giving and taking. I believe you can benefit from this dynamic, too. People like to be asked to help and will help you—just as you'll want to help others.

It may seem a bit too otherworldly to simply be open to whatever happens—even if your introduction doesn't pan out, or the guidance you get isn't spot on. But it's imperative to be able to see beyond the immediate outcome, and not to feel guilty for trying. Keep trying.

Playing a Long Game

In cultivating your loose-touch connections, remember that a network doesn't appear all at once. Meeting and adding contacts is organic, and slow. It takes steady work. You can see why it helps to make a daily (or at least very consistent) habit of sending out a few messages, greetings, and forwarded stories, jokes, and so on. Here's a story about the long game from my own past. Years ago, I met a young PR staffer at a startup whom I'll call Jenny. Her boss, who had been a colleague earlier at Google, brought the young woman to meet and talk with me about how to develop a company blog. As we each changed jobs and traded friendly tweets or notes now and again, Jenny and I kept in (very) loose touch over the next few years. We've actually never sat down face to face since that first meeting. Fast forward: today Jenny is a partner at a venture capital (VC) firm. Last year she introduced one of her firm's companies to me in hopes that I could help them with content strategy. I was appreciative and took on their project. I've told Jenny I'd like to thank her for the referral with a drink or meal—but even if we don't get around to it, our loose tie remains strong.

TRY IT OUT: Build Loose Touch into Your Day

Ten minutes a day building your loose-touch habit can keep you in touch with an awful lot of people. That's a small amount of effort for what is potentially a lot of payoff, in good feelings if not in immediate outcomes. Whether you're the giver or the receiver in need, you'll get a sense of satisfaction either way.

Make it a morning warmup.
My morning ritual of checking email and my news feeds is a way to limber up for the workday. As I scan the headlines, I'll share a story or two that I know are of interest to people I haven't been in touch with along with a short note: "This made me think of you. What's your take? And how are you?"

Keep a running to-do list.
Part of staying in loose touch is simply following up on encounters you've had. After your conversation or meeting, think about what you wanted to pass along, and who came to mind that you'd like to reach out to. Add them to your list and get the satisfaction of crossing that task off later.

Close out the day with gratitude.
Send out a couple of "thinking of you" notes to people you've enjoyed meeting or would like to catch up with, or to even start a new conversation with someone you've just met. It's a nice way to plant the seed of connection that might yield a response as soon as the next day.

For Mutual Benefit

Let me give you another example of how loose touch can work: in this case, how someone uses it with me. Recently I was introduced by a former colleague to a woman, let's call her Michelle, looking for a new position in employee communications. She'd been in her current job for quite a few years, and as a result, she said, she'd let go of her network—she hadn't maintained loose touch with others, and recognized that was a problem. I introduced her to a few contacts I know in her field and wished her luck. She continues to send me short updates on her progress, and when I see stories about employee communications, I forward them to her with a quick note: "Thinking of you, hope all's well." That's it. We don't need to have another meeting. She knows I'm thinking of her, and it's clear I'm on her mind, too. She is meeting people as she pursues new opportunities and expands her thinking, and has built up her network. Here's hoping she won't let it fade away!

One more story about mutual benefit. A few years ago, a British fellow called Ian Sanders asked me a question on Twitter. I responded and, naturally, took a look at his Twitter profile. I liked what I saw (in part it read, "Creative consultant, storyteller, author. Fuelled by coffee, curiosity, walking"), so I followed him back. Ian, who lives near London, helps energize organizations and teams around doing their best work. When I later planned a trip to London, I suggested we meet. We did, have even met a second time, and remain in occasional—loose!—touch. In person, we had time to converse about our approaches to consulting and how we work with groups. I've introduced him to journalists and consultants with whom he's developed relationships; he's inspired me to consider new perspectives about working with clients. We pass along tidbits via Twitter Messages, and each of us considers the other to be a friendly and useful contact, and even a friend.

It's Who You Know

Loose touch works especially well for maintaining contacts you already have. It's how I stay in touch with dozens of people, many of them former colleagues (remember all that job-hopping I mentioned?). I will share tidbits seen on Twitter, or other news of mutual interest. By "share," I mean send along a brief greeting and a link to something interesting to read or watch. Remember how I said we have more ways to do this today than ever before? If you are a regular on LinkedIn, you can keep in loose touch with your contacts via private messages. So too with Twitter or Facebook direct messages, or private messaging on Slack or Instagram—it just depends on which services you already like, and use, and which ones your contacts use. We'll explore these services in more detail in chapter 6.

I'm also a big believer in connecting around shared interests, which are fertile ground for loose-touch moments, even with professional contacts. For example, my friend Erika is a dog lover, and also a fervent promoter of good customer experience. We often send each other hilarious dog GIFs, or we have a virtual laugh over the latest corporate mishandling of customers. Sometimes we do this via Twitter Messages, and sometimes in a private group we share on Slack. Occasionally interspersed with our momentary messaging about dogs and whatever else, one of us will pass along a workshop invitation or a lead for consulting work. All of this is exactly what I mean by keeping in loose touch.

Similarly, I keep up online with a diaspora of friends from Google, many of whom have moved on to work at lots of other companies. We share the kind of kinship many former coworkers enjoy, and that leads to sending around funny or peculiar news items about our old employer, or one of its competitors. There are times when I might send the news link accompanied only by ¯_(ツ)_/¯ (a shrug); it's not uncommon to get back a 👍 ("Okay") in return. Voilà! We just had a loose-touch moment. It could lead to a conversation, or it might not till later. Though such exchanges are virtual, the effect is very much like that of meeting at the neighborhood pub now and again for a quick round. Twenty-five years ago, sociologist Ray Oldenburg argued for the idea of a "third place" besides home and work that occupied human activity and fostered community. Today many people (including me) would include online spaces, in addition to the local coffee bar, as being a kind of third place.

Business professor David Burkus's book *Friend of a Friend* zeroes in on the idea that people you already know, especially those who are weak ties, are the ones best suited to help you. As he observes, "When we have a career setback . . . we tend to only tell a close circle of friends who may or may not be able to help. . . . Instead, we ought to go to our weak and dormant ties, tell them our story, and see what opportunities they have. Even better, we ought to start a regular practice of re-engaging with our weak and dormant ties." That's what keeping in loose touch is about.

It's a Small World After All

One of the best results of asynchronous communication, especially in our always-on world, is that our personal contacts can be anywhere. You may already have friends in other parts of the world, and a growing number of us also work across time zones, and even continents, with customers, clients, and colleagues. Each one of these people represents an opportunity for you to expand your network—all it takes is your sense of curiosity and openness to go beyond routine contact. Using video chat tools like Zoom, Skype, or Google Hangouts (all of which automatically set meeting times to your time zone), or WhatsApp for talk and text, it's never been easier or more seamless to get in touch or stay in touch across many time zones. We're not far from a time when having one employer in a single location, dressing for work, commuting on roads, or being assigned a fixed desk will seem very quaint (and much less desirable). As the world shrinks, your loose-touch network grows in value.

Boundaries Matter, Too

The good news, as we've established, is that it's easier than ever to stay in touch with many people. The downside might be a proliferation of invitations and questions and coffee dates you *don't* want. After all, the whole point of keeping in loose touch is that it's not a burden. The more obligations you end up with, the less chance you have of keeping things loose, or keeping up.

If in response to a simple "how are you?" note you sent, you get an invitation to meet at 2:00 p.m. next Thursday for a meeting with someone you don't know well about . . . well, it's not clear what—you're absolutely within your rights to put it off. You can delay for a while, until you'd genuinely like to meet—or you can delay forever, especially if you feel unequipped to help much. I've had slight acquaintances reach out, eager to join Google, ask me to meet for coffee to talk about the company. Much as I'd like to be helpful, thirty thousand more people have joined since I left. My information isn't that current, so usually I'd rather not commit to a meeting. Instead, I rely on a boundary: I'll send an email with a couple of paragraphs about my broad impressions, perhaps include a recent article that's relevant, and sign off with "good luck," which is genuine.

In this ever-growing web of people with whom to have (some) contact, it is really important to respect boundaries around familiarity, time, and the nature of the request.

And now, having advised you about keeping boundaries, I want to say again, in the spirit of openness, if your curiosity is at all piqued by a random connection request, consider saying "yes" (or at least, "why not?") more often. Some number of casual meetups without a clear agenda will yield wonderful fruit.

"You Were on My Mind"

I've been talking about the value of quick and simple exchanges. The effect of these is simply this: each one puts you into someone's consciousness for a few minutes, and vice versa. These moments serve as a bit of connective tissue ("we have this in common"), a marker of your ongoing relationship.

I should note that the impetus behind creating a loose-touch habit is not very different than a tactic salespeople have had for years: the tickler file. Salesfolk and business development pros often create "ticklers" to remind themselves to get in touch with clients or prospects again. Sales pros I know use ticklers to reflect the clients' interests back to them, and to signal that they are still top of mind.

Loose touch is like a tickler—except that it's not pinned to a sales target and doesn't need a defined outcome. Both ticklers and loose-touch moments are meant to instill ongoing interest and capture any opportunities that might emerge *because of that contact*.

Through a mutual friend, I recently met Julie Schlosser, whom I mentioned earlier. As usual these days, Julie and I were introduced by email, through which we scheduled a call to talk. A former journalist, Julie is now an entrepreneur running an online business for social good—that is, part of her product sales support worthy nonprofit causes. Our mutual friend put us together because she noticed that we are two habitual connectors who maintain loose touch with many people. And we quickly discovered that we do share a habit of reaching out to our brain trust for advice now and again.

Julie believes that one reason she does this easily is because one of her most fruitful networks is a group of women she worked with at Time Inc. years ago, at her first "real" journalism job. Looking back, she says, "It was such a great collegial environment, not competitive like other media outlets. We all helped each other. It was collaborative from the start. We're not always in touch, but I still depend on them. When I ask myself how to tackle this next business challenge, I can call or email a dozen women to ask, 'Do you like this idea? How should I move forward?' It's usually feedback I'm looking for, but they often want to introduce me to other friends or contacts who might be able to help me reach my goal. And the other women do the same when they have problems to solve."

In describing her circle, Julie touches on the main tenets of keeping in loose touch: by definition, you do it intermittently, not constantly, and there's an organic quality that works for everyone. When I asked what drives her to not only connect but stay in touch over time, Julie said, "It goes back to the basics of being a good person, being a good neighbor. You should always be looking out for your friends and former colleagues and neighbors. If you're a good person, you are always ready to help them—and then it's easy to receive or ask for help later."

Now think about who you keep in loose touch with. I bet some are regulars in your life, and some are your "weak ties"—people you know less well. As we'll see in the next chapter, they, too, have great value.

The Value of Weak Ties

Weak ties are one of the keys to the future of work in organizations today and new tools enable employees to build these ties.

—*Jacob Morgan*

The notion of "weak ties"—people you know very slightly at best, perhaps worked with briefly or met through a friend—was developed by Stanford University sociologist Mark Granovetter. His much-cited 1973 research paper, "The Strength of Weak Ties," advanced the idea that in certain fields, the connections between people that are less direct, less obvious, less robust, actually proved to be a better resource for finding a new job than were strong connections. One key finding is a fairly simple idea: "Those to whom we are weakly tied are more likely to move in circles different from our own and will thus have access to information different from that which we receive."

It's true: *We don't know who has the information we might need.* Our chances increase if we reach out beyond our usual circle of contacts, because *other* people will have more, different, and unknown-to-us information. In his paper, Granovetter captured the ironic truth about weak ties—and why they should be a key part of your network: "It is remarkable that people receive crucial information from individuals whose existence they have forgotten."

Exactly. People we don't know well may unlock a puzzle for us. Someone you overlapped with at a previous job but didn't work with. Your neighbor's friend at the barbecue. Someone with whom you share a conference panel. Your mom's caretaker's daughter. Any of these can be weak ties—someone whose own knowledge, network, or idea gets you in a new door, or persuades you to consider another company or a different role outside of what you'd normally consider. By the way, "weak tie" is in no way a critical term. You have them, and you are also one yourself. (I'm somebody else's weak tie, too.) The point here is that people further from your daily orbit can be central to your efforts. Your weak ties are people to include when you are reaching out with questions, need perspective, seek introductions and advice, or want a bit of professional camaraderie.

> People further from your daily orbit can be central to your efforts.

Make Room for Serendipity

Here's a story to inspire you about the power of weak ties. Esther Landau is a seasoned nonprofit development director in San Francisco. After a stint of nearly ten years as fundraiser for an international arts education program, she began the hunt for a new position. She applied all the usual ways—submitting resumes, writing cover letters, taking interviews—for the most suitable openings she could find. Working her LinkedIn contacts, she also set up informational interviews with people in organizations that interested her. But after a few months of looking, and despite her solid credentials, Esther wasn't finding the right fit.

Meanwhile, in another part of her life, Esther was a regular at a local folk-dance club—a weekly meetup of people from all different backgrounds who enjoy learning dances from around the world. One evening during a break, Esther mentioned her search to a fellow dancer, who told her about an opening at the social service nonprofit where she worked. Esther had never worked in the social services sector, but the mission of the organization sounded interesting. Although the opening, for an assistant director, was a step or two below her pay grade, she decided to apply. After a few lively interviews, Esther was offered a higher-level position: the director's job. As it turns out, this was a perfect fit of her personality and skills to the organization and its mission.

If this story sounds familiar to you, that's because it happens a lot. This is serendipity at work: the chance meeting, the offhand comment, the story over drinks, the online post you published in a hurry—any of these can lead to a good outcome.

Weak ties might be people you only know slightly, from past experiences, or they might even be strangers. In a profile of Margit Wennmachers—a storied partner at the well-known VC firm Andreessen Horowitz—*Wired* reporter Jessi Hempel detailed Margit's openness to meeting with, and helping, people she didn't know. In one instance, Margit was introduced to a tech executive who asked for her help to deal with a potentially negative story that was about to appear. "The guy wasn't part of her firm, or even connected to one of its portfolio companies," Hempel writes. "But he could be important one day. Maybe Apple will acquire his company, and she'd have a friend at Apple. Maybe he'll start a new company and come to Andreessen for funding. She calls people like this guy 'the outside nodes of the network,' and considers them strategic relationships that extend her reach."

You might think her decision to spend time with this fellow is both transactional and strategic, and that may be true. But it's also true that Margit knew her effort might not lead anywhere.

The key is that she didn't put any conditions on helping him; she just did it.

Step Away from Narrow Notions

I sometimes have the experience of attempting to help people who want fresh leads in order to land a new job, but they can be a bit too literal about what they are willing to take. I can understand a single-minded focus, especially if the seeker has a deadline looming, such as a job that's going away. People needing job guidance are looking for a fix—a seamless "in" to the perfect job at a dream company. They don't want to be deterred by potential speed bumps that weak ties might represent. But really, weak ties may be exactly the right accelerator.

Here's a cautionary tale about that. A friend I'll call Ron is an experienced corporate lawyer who's eager to take his next step, into a general counsel role. But Ron puts a lot of conditions on that dream. His checklist about a future company has these requirements: it's under five years old, but already making money; it's big enough to do business internationally; it has a few hundred (not tens, not thousands) employees; it's on a solid pre-IPO path; and oh, yes: the office is within ten miles of his home. Good wish list, right? Sadly, for Ron, it all adds up to a near impossibility, even among Silicon Valley's endless proliferation of startups. (In fact, very few companies can meet all of these conditions.) I offered to introduce Ron to a friend who also has a legal background, and is a COO, knowing that their conversation could spark new ideas about Ron's options. But he quickly dismissed my suggestion. He was fixated on being a general counsel at that mythical startup. He could not see the value of talking to someone not currently in that exact same role, or at that dream company already. I knew that the COO (who is extremely well-connected) would know of many companies and executives for Ron to meet—people who, upon meeting Ron, might have sped up their search for a general counsel. Who knows where that conversation might have gone? Not Ron, who passed on the meeting because *he limited himself to what he already knew, or thought he knew.* Guess what? He's still looking. I hate it when this happens—and it doesn't need to.

I'm telling you this story to encourage you to be more open as you think about new opportunities and directions for yourself. Don't be like Ron and rule out encounters that might be informative. In most any career-related search, people you already know, especially your close friends, are not likely to be your best resources. Though they can (and should) absolutely cheer you on, it's the weak ties—more remote, very occasional, not obvious—who are likely to provide breakthrough leads. That's why I'm preaching a bit about being open to meetings, conversations, and introductions you hadn't considered as being vital to your search. I've been surprised myself by the impact that more distant connections can have. I was recruited to Twitter by a friendly acquaintance I would characterize as a weak tie—someone I shared a friend with, and who I saw no more than once a year. After I joined Twitter, I gave back, in a sense, by referring five weak ties of my own—all people I'd met recently or knew only slightly. Every one of them was eventually hired. I hope they, too, have passed on the favor by referring their own weak ties.

Your Personal Ecosystem

My formative years in Silicon Valley have taught me about the value of a personal network and weak ties, especially over time. In her book *Troublemakers: Silicon Valley's Coming of Age*, historian Leslie Berlin captures my experience when she writes that some of Silicon Valley's global renown "has rested on personal connections and collaboration that transcend(s) companies, industries and generations." I would add that any personal network is made up partly of people you don't know very well, but whom over time are part of your ecosystem (as you are part of theirs).

Here's the thing, though: you don't need to be in Silicon Valley to make new contacts, *which will include plenty of weak ties*. Thirty years ago, the region might have been at the forefront of personal networking and job fluidity, but no longer. Today the work scene in the United States broadly shares these characteristics: in a 2015 study of how LinkedIn members found new jobs, the data showed that besides big tech categories (software, hardware, wireless, games), political organizations, management consulting, the film industry, and finance, among others, tend to hire a larger proportion of people via employee networks—that is, people you know or people they know—rather than simply random applications. As the study notes, "Whether you're looking for an opportunity at a growing startup or an established enterprise, networking is going to make a difference . . . the percent of hires that come from employee networks is roughly the same regardless of company size."

Collecting People Along the Way

In 1985, and still fairly new to San Francisco, I took a job in a young industry I could scarcely have imagined before arriving: computer magazines. A sea of them had appeared, virtually overnight, to serve the burgeoning adoption of personal computers. Right away, I began to meet scores of people who would become weak or strong contacts, all a part of growing my network. Three factors in particular fed the young technology industry, and today these same factors influence the much larger world of work:

- **Frequent job changes.** Those heady early days of personal computing are where I first noticed that people my age changed jobs, and even career trajectories, way more often than I thought possible. My Depression-era parents defined success as a stable, long-term job with insurance, two weeks' vacation, and incremental pay raises. My mom in particular had a notably stable career: she worked thirty-five years for one organization and got a nice pension. They both tried to teach me the importance of that stability—but in my world there was no penalty, and there was often success, because of moving around. A 2013 report by the consulting firm Accenture about frequency of job changes in Silicon Valley IT companies showed that although loyalty to an employer is high by national standards, loyalty to coworkers is even higher: "The name of the company they work for is, in some ways, an ancillary detail. That's one reason why people are willing to switch readily from one company to another. . . . People in Silicon Valley behave more like independent contractors, moving from job to job. The result is a highly mobile talent base."

- **People move around but stay connected.** With the steady pace of new companies (one begets another, is sold, or folds), comes the chance to build on your existing network of contacts. In fact, it's considered part of your currency: *Is she well-connected? Does he have good contacts?* It's standard practice in the technology ecosystem to keep up with people you know who work for competitors; keep an eye on corporate moves; recruit people you know (and be recruited); and help those you like, however slightly, make a move. All of this occurs through your network. The Accenture study also notes that "nurturing and participating in peer networks also contributes to the Valley's cooperative atmosphere. . . . More than anywhere else, networking with colleagues inside and outside [a Silicon Valley] organization is essential to their success. Not surprisingly, many also rely on their networks rather than headhunters when looking for a new job."

- **The need to retool your skills is constant.** In 1965, Intel cofounder Gordon Moore had a technical insight about how quickly computer speed and capacity would grow that became known as Moore's Law. Technology journalist and author John Markoff observes that Moore's Law means "nothing stays the same for more than a moment; no technology is safe from its successor . . . if you're not running on what became known as 'Internet time,' you're falling behind." Of course, in the years since Moore's Law took effect the incessant pace of technology development has affected every kind of industry; no one can rely on past connections and expertise alone. It's become more critical than ever to adapt and learn new skills very quickly—and that leads to making new acquaintances and seeking guidance from more people, and more kinds of people, than you might have needed to previously.

TRY IT OUT: Discover Your Weak Ties

If you still need convincing that weak ties matter, here's a list of some people who are among my own weak ties. Your list will vary, of course; ideally, it will reflect similar breadth. Mine includes, but is not limited to:

- people I've hired, people I've failed to hire
- people I've managed, and former managers of mine

- people I've met through mutual friends
- conference-goers
- kindred wordsmiths, writers, editors (i.e., people who share professional interests)
- early internet-era cohorts (old-timers have a special bond)
- people I've met through Twitter or LinkedIn
- college friends, and much-younger alums who found me on LinkedIn
- scads of former colleagues from virtually every place I've worked
- journalists I respect
- former consulting clients
- dog people (rescuers, walkers, trainers)
- fellow volunteers at nonprofits

I hope you don't think of your contacts as just one heterogeneous mass of names. It's not. We all reach out, cultivate, or go dormant with a shifting cast of people all the time, which reflects how we actually operate in life. Nurturing a web of people you already know, used to know, or want to know provides you with a steady supply of your own weak ties—so that you always have someone to call on.

PART TWO

YOUR ONLINE TOOLKIT

Humans want and need connection, and the internet is the ultimate connection machine.

—*Daniel Weitzner*

– 5 –

Blending the Personal and Professional

> We should see ourselves as a whole and integrated
> person, not as someone splintered into a million
> tiny pieces that must be kept isolated.
> —*Rebecca Fraser-Thrill*

An eon ago, people sometimes added a line or two on their CV or resume about their hobbies and interests, which signaled to hiring managers that applicants had a life beyond the office. It was meant to give more dimension to people you might end up working with. Today there are lots of ways to learn more about you than your education and employment history; recruiters check on candidates' social media accounts as a matter of course—not only LinkedIn, but the other discoverable services you might use, such as Instagram, Tumblr, Twitter, or Facebook.

As Cory Fernandez acknowledges in a *Fast Company* article, "It's tricky balancing professionalism with personality, especially when you use social media to share funny memes and catch up with friends in addition to showcasing your expertise." Yes, it is tricky—but I think it's time we all get over the idea that our personal and professional lives can be kept in completely separate silos. Besides, recruiters and hiring managers want to get a sense of you to understand whether you are likely to work well with, and complement, the existing team.

Given my years of interviewing candidates, I understand this thinking. A spirit of collegiality on teams should not be the same as "culture fit," which has become infamous as a kind of shorthand for "hire more people like us." Obviously, doing that stifles diversity. Few of us want to work with automatons who are all business all the time; we enjoy working with people who easily reveal, and share, something of their personal passions and interests. (And it's always more interesting if they're not the same as ours!)

At this point, I can practically feel some readers bristling: "My personal interests are none of your business! I hate our tell-all culture! I'm very private!" Bear with me here as I give you some good news from the front lines of corporate HR. I asked Rosemary Fantozzi, an HR director at security software company Symantec (who describes herself as an introvert) about the issue of "culture fit." She told me her professional circle has gravitated away from that idea toward seeking "cultural contributors"—people who enrich a company's culture by reflecting their own deep-seated values rather than needing to "fit" with the existing group, or excelling at social activities. As Rosemary put it, "This is me at my best: my values + my skills + the company's business need." This approach to employees-as-contributors is well suited to introverts. (We can demonstrate our values, just don't ask us to over-share personal traits.) As an introvert, there is a good deal I, too, keep to myself, especially at the office. Even so, I know that sharing some of my opinions and interests enhances my ability to connect. That's why I want make the case for a little blending of your personal and professional selves. It's something you can absolutely control, and I believe it will help you in several ways over time.

In a 2017 article, educator Kerry Gallagher made note of the "social media threshold" many people are crossing today. Her examples of this crossover for teachers who grapple with the personal/professional connection will seem familiar:

- Teachers have relationships with others that started online "yet are very real," in which they inspire each other via social media, and occasionally meet at conferences. This leads them to share "non-professional information that good friends normally share."
- Some of these professional acquaintances ask to follow/befriend one another. [It may mean] "someone from Twitter sends a friend request on Facebook or follower request on Instagram or Snapchat."
- On the professional front, a teacher's guest post, Twitter chat, or accomplishments of their students "is so exciting that they can't help but share it on their personal feed."

Gallagher, a digital learning specialist in Massachusetts, is also director of K-12 education for ConnectSafely.org, a nonprofit that provides safety and privacy tips to parents and teachers. She notes that for most of us, our social media accounts "include family, friends from [school], neighborhood friends, colleagues from work . . . and more. Often, people from one category are also part of another. Real life is messy. Creating clean social media categories will also eventually get messy. . . . I'm all for sharing your moments of success, struggles, and lessons learned, and the best resources that have helped you along the way."

The Rise of Sharing

As I write this, LinkedIn is fifteen years old; Facebook is fourteen; Twitter is twelve; Instagram is eight. In less than a generation, we've crossed that chasm of keeping personal and public selves more or less separate. We're generally comfortable seeing, and sharing, opinions, life events, ideas, jokes, images, and news well beyond our circle of family and friends. Susan Etlinger, an industry analyst who writes about the impacts of technology on people, observed that "In the old days, we had pretty limited ways to interact with each other, whether in person or online, and the distinctions between 'personal' and 'professional' were clearer. In today's online world, it's more of a continuum."

With its two billion users, Facebook dominates the landscape, and was the first large-scale network designed around the notion that people would share personal stories and information. Facebook's primacy today is one of the key reasons we've become accustomed to posting—revealing—personal information about ourselves to a growing number of people, reaching beyond our immediate circles.*

From Facebook to Goodreads, from Slack to Reddit to Snapchat and more, we've come to expect that whatever our interests, our personal and professional expressions run along a continuum—one that we can control. In chapter 6, we'll take a closer look at several social media services and how to make the best use of those you prefer.

Being Three-Dimensional

Even among powerful business executives, politicians, journalists, celebrities, and other public figures, it's become the norm

---

* As I write this in the spring of 2018, Facebook has experienced perhaps its most serious public crisis to date, a highly charged collision between its service and geopolitics. New revelations have emerged almost daily about the company's lax policies about third-party access to user data, especially through a data-mining business called Cambridge Analytica. The firm extended its reach into Facebook user data without the consent or necessary security measures in place to protect the privacy of millions of Facebook users. This is the most recent chapter of a long-simmering discussion about how large technology-based services may aggregate user data for the purpose of targeted marketing (including political messaging and campaigns)—all of which delve into complex legal and policy issues well beyond the scope of this book. The upshot is that our understanding about what is public or private is muddier than ever.

to showcase more of what we believe, what we find funny or wrenching, family photos, what we endorse or criticize via our various channels. TV drama impresario Shonda Rhimes tweeted her praise to the judge presiding over the 2018 case against serial sexual abuser Larry Nassar. Bill Gates shared a chapter of his favorite new book with his Facebook followers. Journalist and CNN correspondent Jake Tapper tweets on behalf of his dog, @winstontapper.

Other familiar examples are from executives publicly sharing what were once considered very personal experiences. In 2016, Christi Shaw, then head of the US division of pharma giant Novartis, initially said she was stepping down for "personal and family reasons"—but quickly saw that familiar phrase is commonly understood as meaning "she's been fired." She went public with more detail: her sister had bone marrow cancer and needed a full-time caretaker for a clinical trial. The previous year, Google CFO Patrick Pichette publicly posted a long statement about why he had decided to leave the company after seven years: "I could not find a good argument to tell Tamar [his wife] we should wait any longer for us to grab our backpacks and hit the road [and] celebrate our last 25 years together by turning the page and enjoy a perfectly fine mid-life crisis full of bliss and beauty . . ."

Most famously, perhaps, Sheryl Sandberg has publicly posted several times about the aftermath of having suddenly lost her husband, Dave Goldberg. Similarly, Mark Zuckerberg has confided on Facebook about the pain he and his wife, Priscilla Chan, suffered through three miscarriages. Skeptics might believe that these two powerful executives are simply showcasing their own service to the world; I'd argue that they have chosen to address these very personal matters publicly because they, too, are in this moment of blending the personal and professional.

Of course, people who are already in the public eye are likely to risk less than some of us when they share a life experience or an opinion that is outside their professional selves. Even so, every day, we see posts, and stories, from all kinds of people about a vast range of personal experience and life changes. Most are not heart-stoppingly serious: the personal-professional blend is more likely to be about everyday activities, ideas, and pleasures.

Your instinct may be to hold back from sharing on social media in an attempt to keep whatever tiny bit of privacy still exists in the world, or keep a superclean public profile—but that may work against you. With no identifiable or relatable traits, you may appear inauthentic to some. Even we introverts (and others who lean toward personal privacy) can find a happy medium in what we share about ourselves.

> Your instinct may be to hold back from sharing on social media in an attempt to keep whatever tiny bit of privacy still exists in the world, or keep a superclean public profile—but that may work against you.

My former colleague Tim Fisher is someone who recently began to appreciate this personal-professional blending. A long-time pro in both business development and customer experience strategy, Tim says he "had a real hang-up when it came to mixing the personal and professional. I simply avoided business relationships with people I knew primarily through my personal life. I worried about what might happen to our relationship if the business side didn't work out well, and I worried about how I'd feel in trying to sell them something they weren't interested in."

So Tim kept his personal life and work life separate. But

over time, as his professional network grew, Tim found himself with "hundreds and hundreds of relationships" that were now harder to define: "There were scores of people I had worked with, or clients who had hired me, who fell into a unique category, maybe 'work-friends.' We probably didn't talk very often, and truthfully, I knew we'd probably never work again as closely as we did when we first met." Was his vow not to do business with friends even valid anymore, now that so many of his friendships had evolved from work contacts? He began to wonder why he was even bothering to preserve these connections at the same time as he was making them off-limits for deeper connections. It took Tim moving to a new company "to fully embrace the potential of the work-friend network and deepen these relationships."

Today Tim recognizes his "work-friends" as "a large group of people who know me, trust me, and hopefully respect me—exactly the things people are looking for in a business partner. People want to hire or partner with the people they know, like, and trust." The way he sees it now, "It took me awhile to get out of my own way. But my work-friend network is now one of the first places I turn to learn something new."

Tim's discovery dovetails with this now-common public blending of interests and opinions—so much so that it now may seem inauthentic to strictly adhere to professional-only expressions. Even if you don't know all of your social media contacts socially, by now you are undoubtedly accustomed to seeing vacation and wedding pics, baby news, graduations, the arrival of the new pet (or sad departure of an old one), as well as news about jobs or promotions, commingled in your feeds.

You Are in Control

Longtime marketing educator and author Ann Handley has also written about this blend: "People do business with people," she says, "not faceless, soulless edifices. Don't you want your prospects and customers online to have an opportunity to get to know you, just as your friends, colleagues and contacts in real life do?" Ann consciously balances the personal and professional on her two Twitter accounts, @annhandley and @marketingprofs; the latter is her business identity. She doesn't share exactly the same information in both places.

In an interview for this book, Ann explained that for @marketingprofs, "There's an extra layer of me questioning, 'does this make sense?'" since that account represents a brand, a service, and a team—not just her. To the larger point about personalization, she observes that the "inherent promise" of social media, and one of its key values, is to show that humans are textured, and have dimensions.

> You don't have to reveal too much of yourself to be three-dimensional.

When I asked her how to answer people who are cautious about exposing parts of their lives, Ann counseled, ". . . think of personalizing your brand, not getting personal. The former means showing that you're a real human being. You have a point of view, real character, a personality. The latter is sharing details that are intimate or too specific to you to have relevance for the larger community." For those of you who bristle at thinking of yourself as a "brand"—I really hear you on this, as it can seem like jargon run amok. Avoid the term if you like, but consider that what you share about your whole self helps you to be more three-dimensional—and you don't have to reveal too much. Doing that with thoughtfulness can enhance your reputation, which, you won't be surprised to know, can lead to more opportunities.

Each of us has to determine what that line is in relation to our livelihoods and aspirations. Through her business presence on Twitter, Ann says she really enjoys one real-world effect in particular: as a frequent traveler and speaker, she delights in meeting Twitter followers wherever she appears. It's a phenomenon she refers to as a "pre-union"—you've already met online, now you're meeting in person.

TRY IT OUT: Put Yourself Out There (a Little)

When it comes to some celebrities and other over-sharers, it may feel we're living in the age of TMI (too much information). But you *can* extend your online persona—the one people are going to find anyway—without fear of overdoing. In the process, you add color and depth to the impression you give others. Here are some low-stress ways to reveal more of yourself.

- Photo galleries or posts featuring your pets, garden, or vacation spots. (Kids fall under this category if you are comfortable sharing photos of them.)
- Profile headers depicting a favorite image: your sports team of choice, an evocative landscape, artwork, or motto.
- Blogs or posts showcasing your favorite books or authors, music, films, and TV shows.
- Mentions or donation requests supporting causes you care about, such as charity walks and runs, emergency and natural disaster needs, volunteer programs.
- Retro photos with a story. (If not of yourself, then of your city or town, antique gadgets, clothing styles, and the like.)

A New Kind of Social Authenticity

Our public personae are fair game today not only for recruiters, but for lots of others: competitors, board member–seekers, reporters, law enforcement, old classmates, the randomly curious. For many of us, it's become second nature to look for people online through one or more of these platforms, see what they're up to, how we might be connected. It's become rarer than ever to find *no* online footprint for the wide swath of people between 18 and 75. In January 2018, Pew Research reported that 88 percent of 18- to 29-year-olds use social media; 78 percent of 30- to 50-year-olds, and 64 percent of 50- to 64-year-olds. Among the 65-plus crowd, 37 percent are social media users.

There are plenty of legitimate reasons why people don't want to appear much online, even in the relatively staid space of LinkedIn, but the effect is something you want to consider. You're less likely to be under consideration, or in a conversation, if you're not there at all. While we all should take steps to secure facts about ourselves that we truly do not want to be discovered (that new tattoo in a private spot, perhaps, or a scrape with a credit bureau), I wholeheartedly endorse revealing a comfortable level of personal information—your choice as to how much, and what—along with your professional aspirations. Doing that adds the kind of dimensionality we expect in each other; it's how we socialize. Taking this a step further, knowing that your future manager loves to hike or cook is also beneficial to you, if you're on the team or you're at a startup needing to build a team.

The blending of our personal and professional news and perspectives has led to a new kind of *social authenticity*. This is a way to reinforce the idea that each of us is more than the sum of our parts. I think of social authenticity as a credential we obtain through the whole of our self-expression on whichever social networks we use. It's something we each have to spend, share, and save. We do this by affirming the posts and comments of others, cheering on their successes, supporting causes we agree with, and even sometimes mourning their losses, which certainly happen in the real world. If you're not sharing and expressing yourself to some degree, you're missing out on this aspect of nurturing your own network.

Social authenticity has gained a foothold for another reason: the rise of a lot of online sharing and recommendations, around everything from movies and books to travel destinations and local favorites. We're used to reading, and writing, and seeking out opinions and comments about the stuff we care about. Then there are affinity groups and message boards organized entirely online around communities of interest for virtually every kind of medical challenge, social cause, and life event.

You control what you share in a face-to-face conversation; it's not that different on the screen *if* you are thoughtful about what and when to post. (In other words, think twice about sending live updates from that pub crawl or overheated political rally.) In real life we get to choose what we reveal. You are also in charge of what information you put out online. This fuzzier boundary between elements of our lives marks our social authenticity. It has its advantages; a thoughtful approach is a must. The more you share, the more you will get back. This is true in both your personal and professional lives, online and in person.

Make Social Media Work for You

While the internet often connects us one-to-one, it also introduces us to new networks and provides endless opportunities for exploration, learning, and sharing. If we don't want to share, we don't have to share. The best part is: we get to choose.

—*Sarah Granger*

We've been talking about blending personal and professional, especially in an online environment, and how to make that work in ways that you feel comfortable with. My experience tells me that if you're adept at communicating online, you can make meaningful connections well beyond the people you'd be likely to meet in person. You can meet, befriend, and do business with people you may not know in "real" life. ("Real" in quotes here, because these days online life is simply a part of our daily routine.) I've written this chapter to walk you through some specific ways you can develop or strengthen your daily loose-touch habit online. So let's dive into a few of the social platforms, which offer great and varied opportunities to help you stay connected to people you already know, and to connect with people you want to meet.

The internet has long invited us to explore, learn, and share, and through those activities, to connect with others. So it's perfectly suited to—perfect for—introverts. From the comfort of your desk, kitchen table, or favorite coffee bar, you can put yourself in front of prospective employers, reconnect with former colleagues to gather intel on your next move, and meet with people on your terms in your field(s) of interest. The last twenty-five years of internet life has given me value in these ways, especially through the web of connections I've gained. I certainly would never have been able to meet as many people offline as I have online. There are ways for everyone (maybe especially we who would rather stay home on a Saturday night) to make today's social media services work for us.

Much of my work in writing and consulting consists of a daily mix of these things: initiating and responding to email, instant messaging, Google searches, video calls, reading and sending tweets and private messages, LinkedIn research, texting, and a few side trips to Instagram and Facebook. This is not only how I work; these tasks and habits are how I connect with people to learn new things, consider new ideas, share news, and touch base. You probably do some or most of these things, too. This chapter can help you make better and more efficient use of them in the service of connecting with others.

Susan Etlinger, the industry analyst I mentioned earlier, writes about the impacts of technology on people. She reminded me that in 2006, when Facebook opened its service beyond college students, "there was this tentativeness in the way that people interacted with each other," and observed that it was like "walking into a party where you didn't really know anybody." Over time, as many of us joined in, we became more comfortable in mixing up what we posted and sent around: personal news and photos, new jobs and life changes, political opinions, causes, helping others. Steadily, we went from pokes and jabs to fuller-throated expressions of ourselves. And as we know (maybe all too well), today we're used to blending aspects of our personal lives with our public—our discoverable—selves.

Where you do your connecting and sharing depends on your interests and which social platforms you like to use. In this chapter, we'll look closely at three of them: LinkedIn, Twitter, and Instagram. I focus on these in particular because none of them requires a 1:1 relationship between you and another person; they are each what's called an asymmetrical network. All were designed so that you can connect informally with people you already know, and also discover new people, whose posts, images, comments, and updates you can see and react to. You don't have to know the people you're looking up or following; you can reach out to meet or even just respond without being directly connected. The important idea here is that each one takes you beyond your immediate circle, so that you can easily enter new territory, beyond the familiar, via new contacts.

> Over time, many of us have become more comfortable in mixing up what we post and send around: personal news and photos, new jobs and life changes, political opinions, causes, helping others.

The oldest of these, LinkedIn, was launched in 2003 to help people build their professional networks and get other help with their career aspirations, and it's remained remarkably true to this mission. Twitter was born in 2006 as a kind of free-range short-form public platform—everyone who uses it has a different experience, based on which accounts they follow. One result is that it's very easy to discover and connect with like-minded people on Twitter. The youngest service, Instagram (which is owned by Facebook), is designed to showcase photography and other imagery, serving up an endless stream of visual posts and stories.

It thrives among creators and celebrities of all kinds, as well as many organizations and consumer brands with a visual story to tell.

Most all of the other services that claim a "social" label—meaning that it's easy for people to create, share, and react to words and pictures through the platform—include Facebook, Snap, YouTube, and WhatsApp, to name a few. Social network services are built around your personal contacts who are also on the service, which is in your feed when you first sign up. In each case, you can control the size of your circle—for example, you can manually enter contacts if you don't want to port over your whole address book, or you could choose to link it and then unfollow individuals within your list. Though you can change your settings so that more people (in Facebook's case, friends of friends, or even the public at large) can see what you post, none of these services was designed to be publicly discoverable. That makes them less useful for connecting 1:1 with people you don't already know. They can offer great utility and pleasure but are less relevant to our focus here.

Three Services for Discovering and Connecting

Let's dive into each of these three, any of which can help you keep in loose touch with lots of people you know, want to know, and even should know.

The Most Direct Connection: LinkedIn
Designed with networking at its core.

The biggest, oldest service designed specifically to help job seekers and employers connect, LinkedIn was built with the network effect in mind: "If each of your twenty trusted contacts connected you to twenty more of their own, you could potentially contact more than 150,000 professionals through the people you already know and trust." LinkedIn's features help you to showcase yourself and connect with others. Whether you are looking for new opportunities, want a public profile (so others can find you), want to see recommendations (so you can see who you don't know), want to find People You May Know (as the service's suggestion feature for connecting with weak ties is called), or all of the above, LinkedIn is very good for making and maintaining professional relationships. As founder Reid Hoffman said in a 2009 interview, "People need to talk to people they don't already know in order to get the job done"—"the job" meaning the work of finding connections to hire, be hired, and do business.

What LinkedIn Is Best For

- **Connecting** with people you know or have worked with
- **Getting introduced** to people you want to know
- **Sharing** your ideas through posts and articles
- **Participating** in professional discussions

As Etlinger, the industry analyst, puts it, "At first LinkedIn was all about following public figures like Richard Branson and Bill Gates; now I think it's a lot better at finding 'regular' people—there are people out there who I could learn as much from, whom I don't know, and I don't know that I don't know them." Today more than 500 million career-minded people around the world have made LinkedIn the de facto site for making contacts, finding job leads and open positions, doing research on companies, raising their profiles, and through LinkedIn Groups meeting people with similar professional interests. Pew Research recently reported that about 50 percent of Americans with a college degree use LinkedIn, versus just 9 percent of those with a high school diploma or less.

Companies and recruiters pay LinkedIn to list jobs, find prospects, and vet candidates. This means you should assume that people seeking talent for all kinds of openings poke around constantly on LinkedIn and may look at your profile. Fortunately, LinkedIn will tell you which people or organizations have taken a look: click on the Me icon at the top of your LinkedIn homepage, click on View Profile, and select Who's Viewed Your Profile. It's always a good idea to check out who has visited, as it might spark new ideas about making connections and where to look for openings.

In general, it's best to think of your LinkedIn presence as a kind of active sport—for you to keep an eye on and continue to tweak, and for everyone else on the service who can see your profile among others they're looking up. It's become a handy way to reflect your accomplishments, describe your strengths and aspirations. These days, a LinkedIn URL often takes the place of a resume or CV— and for introverts and others who hate the idea of networking, it's truly a godsend. Without going to a single in-person function, you can have impact and presence in your field, or a field you hope to enter. You can update your account any time you like—revise wording, change your photo, add or delete previous positions. What's more, you can turn off change notifications so that others won't be alerted to your edits until you want them seen—especially important as you revise wording in advance of a new job search. And it's always a good idea to look at the view of your profile that others will see and review your settings to understand how much you want to reveal to nonmembers and search engines, or how to limit your discoverability only to LinkedIn members.

LinkedIn has four key features that are at the heart of its value for building meaningful contacts. They are Profile, LinkedIn Groups, Posts, and, of course, that all-important Connect with others.

LinkedIn Tip #1: Make Your Profile Count

Because it's a place where people in business (or who aim to be, like new grads) look for one another—to recruit and hire, to consult, to learn about potential employers—I encourage people to maintain a current profile. Even if you're happy in your job or in school, it's still good hygiene to review your Profile at least quarterly to see if anything needs refining. People are always looking for advisors, conference speakers, board members, and press sources based on expertise. Why not you?

1. **Visit your Settings & Privacy page** to turn off notifications (to others) about changes you're making. (The path on LinkedIn is Me > Settings & Privacy > Privacy > How others see your LinkedIn activity > Change > Sharing Profile Edits > choose Yes or No.)

2. **Frame your Summary** with an eye toward your aspirations: what you want to do next, or your special mix of skills. This is the area where you're most able to craft a message about your overall talents. Even if you're not actively looking, go beyond merely summarizing current and past jobs to paint a picture of your goals and the value of all you bring to the party.

3. **Use your Profile** to describe your current and past responsibilities and accomplishments clearly, so that viewers who aren't familiar with the shorthand used in your field can understand how your work might apply to new roles.

4. **Update and detail recent projects**, as well as any published work and conference appearances to get attention and traction. Link to specific talks, videos, and articles wherever possible. If you're just starting out, you want to get in the habit of updating your profile to reflect your career interests, and to start developing connections.

5. **Browse your own connections** from time to time to see who you know who's connected to people looking at your profile. This is where those "small world" networking moments start.

LinkedIn Tip #2: Your Summary Matters—a Lot

While there's no single style for a LinkedIn Profile, I recommend using a conversational tone where you can. It's especially valuable for the Summary, which is at the top of your profile. That's the first stop for many visitors and the fastest way to give people a sense of what you're about. You can encapsulate your accomplishments to date at a high level here, but also (or even instead) frame a bigger picture about what you *want* to do. That's especially important for anyone looking to begin a career, change fields, or return to a career after a break. Think of the Summary as a way to pre-introduce yourself to people you'd like to connect with. If you don't have a lot of experience, spend time on the Summary to give us your view of the world and how you'd like to improve it through your passions (which you should tell us about!).

Here are a few examples from among my contacts that feature a high-level Summary. Though different, each of them signals very quickly what that person's skills and interests are. First, some independent consultants:

Kate is the founder of Hedgehog + Fox, a strategic communications consultancy that works with organizations on public relations strategy, media and presentation training, and executive thought-leadership development. We bring human voices to complex companies, helping founders and executives to connect with their stakeholders using authentic and compelling messages. *[Kate Mason]*

Three decades ago, in an era when no one believed anyone would buy B2B software without an in-person meeting, I designed and built Oracle's inside sales group—now a multi-billion dollar global sales organization. Today, my team of experts at Reality Works Group is helping companies build revenue-generating businesses of the future. *[Anneke Seley]*

Strategist. Storyteller. Change agent. I'm an expert at defining a brand's strategy and identity, then bringing it to life in unique and inspiring ways—through engaging storytelling, immersive experiences, and interactive environments. The intersection of strategy and design is my favorite place to be . . . and I love launching things—brands, teams, products, initiatives, new ways of working. *[Cathy Girr]*

And here are a few people who have a history of full-time in-house roles:

A dynamic, passionate, and experienced finance professional with expertise in designing, revamping and managing small to mid-sized companies' financial health and systems. *[Nancy Dent]*

Civic and cultural leader with a couple decades of experience leading nonprofits and advancing equitable change. *[Deborah Cullinan]*

I'm passionate about technology's ability to improve people's lives, which has led me to Twitter, Uber, and Stripe, where I've had operational experience across functional areas including product management, product marketing, sales management, business development, and international expansion. I have an insatiable appetite for learning, having pursued both BS and MBA degrees at Stanford, where I was a Mayfield Fellow and president of Stanford Women in Business. I love languages (spoken or programmed) so much that I've taken classes on eight of them—everything from French to C++. *[Amy Saper]*

Even though these summaries vary considerably, each one offers a broad view of the person's abilities and interests—and wouldn't you like to know any one of them better? Their summaries make them seem approachable. In each case, I want to keep reading.

LinkedIn Tip #3: The All-Important Job Chronology

Next, your LinkedIn chronology—the standard way of enumerating jobs and roles that go beneath your Summary is to write these entries in resume-style language, using a bit of shorthand to convey a sequence of positions and responsibilities. I'd encourage you to be crisp in describing the highlights of each role or project. Where you can, it's really useful to include whatever is measurable—and that probably applies mostly to people in businesses where metrics are part of the daily routine. Here are a few examples that do a good job of summarizing scope or accomplishment:

- End-to-end HR global responsibility for 2,000 employees (17% of org and growing) in 20+ countries. *[Rosemary Fantozzi]*

- Early state product incubation and partnerships across a range of Google products. Led 100+ strategic partnerships and outreach trips in Iraq, Afghanistan, Pakistan, Palestine. *[Mary Grove]*
- Implemented the company's initial mobile-first, global site redesign increasing product page traffic by 41% and improving conversion rates by more than 2%. *[Stephen Fox]*

If you don't have anything measurable you can tout (and many jobs do not), offering a clear explanation of your specialties and level of responsibility is an absolute tonic in the sea of job jargon out there. Here are some very nice, and concise, examples:

- I lead the visual and UX redesign of our pro resource center, several product launch and feature pages, and various other creative touch points (videos, emails, illustrations, etc.). *[Brier Avril]*
- Hired as marketing and communications expert to help early stage founders with positioning, naming, messaging, go-to-market strategy, and launch execution. *[Arielle Jackson]*
- Building on experience in higher education, financial services, digital technology, and nonprofit organizations, I bring fresh eyes to help you move ahead with your design and strategy goals using (mostly) qualitative research methods. *[Nancy Frishberg]*

Finally, for in-between-jobs folks, new grads, and those who have been out of the paid workforce, here's a special shout-out: your job chronology can include volunteer work, educational projects, and even jobs not always considered "professional." (I bet you learned a lot about customer service from waiting tables, or your fundraising experience at your kids' school taught you what it takes to convert interest to tangible support.) Take the immediate experience you've had and think more broadly about how a future employer can benefit from what you know.

LinkedIn Tip #4: Make the Most of Groups

LinkedIn Groups are worth exploring, both to make contacts and also to have a private place (relatively speaking; some groups have thousands of members) to talk about your field, inform others, and learn from them.

To find groups of interest, visit linkedin.com/groups/discover or do a name or keyword search at the top of the LinkedIn site. You'll see write-ups of each group, its size, and a list of your connections who have joined. And there can be a lot of them: current hot topics, such as "content marketing" or "user experience," bring up more than 1,500 results for each. You can't see individual posts until you join, but it's easy enough to join, quit, and rejoin groups once you see how busy (or not) they are and how useful they are. If you're joining groups to expand or change your professional focus, career coach Nancy Collamer suggests that you display the logos of the LinkedIn Groups you've joined in your Profile: "It's a subtle way to reinforce your interest in different fields or companies . . . and an especially valuable tactic if you're trying to shift careers, but don't yet have much relevant experience to display on your Profile."

Here's how to do this: LinkedIn Groups > My Groups > Groups That I'm In > Group Setting > Display Group Logo. (You'll need to do this for each group whose logo you'd like to add.)

Ryan McDougall, a group product manager at LinkedIn, told me that the Groups feature creates "a sense of shared purpose, and that does something valuable: it curates the people. If your question is, 'Hey, I really like your topic. Would you have thirty minutes to talk about . . .'; by putting it in the context of a community, that creates just a little bit more reason to say yes."

Besides the many LinkedIn Groups that reflect professional interests, virtually every kind of affinity—veterans, LGBT, Latinx, and African Americans, among others—are represented. (And there's no need to limit yourself to just one or two of these.) There is a wide range of industry-focused topics covered (retail, medical devices, robotics, real estate are just a few of these). Search on words and phrases to pull up those of interest so you can connect with your tribe(s). Here's how to find Groups that may be of interest:

- From your LinkedIn home page, use the search box to type in the terms you're looking for. The initial results will be across LinkedIn categories, including People, Companies, Content, and More.

- More has a pull-down menu, and you can select Groups there. That's how you see all of those that LinkedIn members have created, and you can read more about each one before joining.

- Once you've joined one or more Groups, you'll see their icons on your Profile—a handy way to indicate some of your interests to people who come across you. Jump into conversations where you feel you can add something, and post about your ideas and especially lessons you've learned. Read through posts of people you admire to get some ideas and approach what you have to say in a spirit of helping others. Other members will take note of your effort, especially over time.

- In other words, Groups are a place to make contact with context, and where you can build credibility by participating in discussions, offering your experience, sharing a helpful article, and by raising or answering questions. In a relatively private space, this activity helps to establish your bona fides and expand your network. (Don't forget to include @ in front of a person's name when you do respond, so they are notified about your mention. It's a goodwill gesture that also encourages more exchange, even with those you're not connected to directly.) As McDougall says, "The nice thing about a conversation is it can start between two people and easily find the third, and the fourth, and the fifth, who are going to add value whether it's insights, opinions, even opportunities, like jobs or gigs."

LinkedIn Tip #5: Raise Your Visibility Through Writing

If you use LinkedIn already, you may have noticed that your home page features a familiar-looking cascade of posts, much like those on Twitter and Facebook, showing news, notes, and information from your LinkedIn contacts and others you follow. And above that feed, there's an invitation for you to "share an article, photo, video or idea." If you choose the article option, you'll get a blank field that resembles the opening screen of a simple word processor, ready for your thoughts. Writing your own posts on LinkedIn is a great way to share your takes on industry news, lessons learned on the job, trend watching, or other professional ideas. Susan Etlinger, the industry analyst I mentioned earlier, praises LinkedIn as being "by far the most useful professional tool" she uses, adding it's "a really great platform for content, and content-driven interaction," so people can follow her based on their interests.

If you post an article from elsewhere, seize the chance to comment on it, and call out people you know to add to the conversation (by linking to their names, they will be notified to take a look at what you've written). These callouts and posts will get you some notice and add to your overall profile and visibility. That, in turn, opens the door to new contacts and conversations.

Though LinkedIn would no doubt like it best if all your posts originated there, you can of course repost articles from your other accounts (your own or your company's blog or Medium page, for example) or other media (magazines, newspapers, professional publications) in order to gain extra readers and attention. If you do that, it's a good idea to address your LinkedIn readers directly, by adding new comments and context at the top. You do this for two reasons: one, to let them know this article has appeared elsewhere; and two, you want to connect directly with your LinkedIn community to share it (and, of course, some of them will pass it along). In this way, more people can learn about you and your ideas or business.

Ready to Start Writing?

Here's a great checklist by LinkedIn marketing staffer Tyrona Heath to get you started on what to write about:

- Why am I writing this now?
- What knowledge, insight, or expertise can I bring that no one else can?
- Do I have an opinion on this topic? Is it clearly laid out? What evidence can I use to support this viewpoint?
- How can I bring the news or latest industry insights into my post? Is there something everyone is talking about that I can incorporate?

LinkedIn Tip #6: Connecting with Others

Just how much does connecting matter on LinkedIn? As with other metrics, quality matters more than quantity, so don't chase the 500 for its own sake—connect with people whose profiles, experience, writings are interesting to you. By the way, LinkedIn only indicates "500+" on all accounts reaching that milestone, no matter how many more connections they have. (You can see your exact number on your own profile.) Today, I have about 3,000 LinkedIn connections, but the number matters less than who I can reach about a specific question I have.

You're certainly not obligated to say yes to all invitations, but it's worth taking a close look at those who want to connect with you. Some can be useful and solid connections in your network; others, not so much, but the trick is, you never know. Right now, I'm sitting on about 150 recent invitations I haven't responded to. When I get invitations from unfamiliar names, I look at their Profiles as well as our mutual connections. If I don't see a compelling reason to add them, I don't take any action; I'll look again later. Sometimes it takes a while to see what value a connection might have, and I don't want to reject an invitation too quickly.

If you don't have a lot of connections, take the time to write a personal note with your request to someone you'd like to link to. Explain that you're interested in their field or specialty, or have questions about their company. A personal message helps the people you're asking decide that they want to help you; they might also find your experience interesting. Your note gives some context that can tip the balance to someone saying yes.

Of course, the lifeblood of LinkedIn is to accept networking requests. I'm all for that in principle, but we know that invitations can be misused, because people have different aims in wanting to connect. When I asked my own friends and contacts what they dislike most about networking, one response was about random requests to connect—specifically on LinkedIn. Here's a representative comment: "I deplore the LinkedIn flavor of networking: 'Even though we've never met, and we're three degrees removed, can you do X for me?' The disregard for the fact that X takes time and requires a genuine connection to be meaningful."

To make meaningful connections, consider these approaches:

- Explore your LinkedIn connections thoroughly to gauge who you know best, even if it takes a few hops to get to the desired person. Along the way you can make contact with others who might be valuable, too, especially if you tell them a bit about what you're looking to do.

- Don't start a request to a stranger by simply asking them to connect you to someone else. (This is the equivalent of *I've glanced at your name tag, and now I'm looking past you for someone more interesting.*) Give some context for your request and acknowledge with gratitude that you know it takes their time and attention.

- Have something meaningful to say as your opener, even if it's simply "I'd like to know more about the work you do/your company." As product manager Ryan McDougall noted, "The best advice for how to reach out on LinkedIn stems from 'be a human being.' If you're asking for something, is there something you can give? Start with a little bit of flattery. That never hurts. And once you have that conversation, you end up top of mind if they are looking for something. That's a way of creating those connections."

Combining an Old-Growth Network and Newcomers

Longtime friend and former colleague Travis Culwell told me an illuminating story about how he used LinkedIn alongside his personal network to land a great new job. A comfortably middle-aged MBA, Travis specializes in marketing and design strategy. After several years as an independent consultant, he decided to seek an in-house position. Knowing this quest could take a while, he maintained his consulting business and client projects as he began the search. He wanted to take his time to thoroughly chase down every lead, which he then proceeded to do.

Through a single conversation with a corporate recruiter who had reached out to him because of his LinkedIn Profile, Travis knew he wasn't interested in the jobs she initially pitched. But during their chat, she happened to mention that the company was forming a new division—more R&D and exploratory in nature than the core business, which piqued his interest. Though there weren't any relevant openings when he first looked into it, he did check LinkedIn to see which of his connections might have a contact there. Voilà! He found a former colleague whom I'll call Marge, who was at the parent company and linked to someone in this fledgling group. Because Marge was what Travis calls a "high value, old-growth" contact—someone he had worked with years before and had stayed loosely in touch with—he could go to her directly for an introduction to the person in his desired group. I love that phrase, "high value, old-growth" to describe core members of your network—people you trust more than most to begin the hunt, often because you've been in the work trenches together. It was easy for Travis to speak with Marge, given their history, but she wasn't clear on how he would fit within the new organization—and she was leaving the company, so couldn't be of much further help.

Travis continued to search among various openings, and a few months later, he took another look on LinkedIn at the growing roster of people now associated with his desired organization. This time he found a weak tie who was actually working there. Once they'd made contact, this acquaintance immediately sensed that Travis would be a good match for a newly posted role. The weak tie moved his resume quickly, which led to a round of phone screens, in-person interviews—and an offer, which Travis accepted. Success! Reality check: this particular process, which involved many paths with many contacts and companies beyond his ultimate target, took the better part of a year. Travis was unfazed, because he understood he was looking for a very particular opportunity.

Your own quest may not take that long, but Travis's story is still instructive. It's a good lesson in how to work both your old-growth contacts, as well as those evolving in your LinkedIn circle over time, and with an eye toward who can help with which parts of a search. LinkedIn made it easy for Travis to keep current on his evolving connections to people related to this new division—a task that would have been difficult, if not impossible, without the service. Beyond that, he relied on his real-life contacts to learn more and make additional connections—all from the comfort of his laptop, right up to the in-person meetings that led to the job offer.

LinkedIn shouldn't be your only tool for making connections and finding good roles, of course. But it *was* designed to level the field enough so that you can find the right people to help, and to help you, and recruiters can find you, too. Ryan, the LinkedIn product manager, notes that founder Reid Hoffman created the company to address the "inefficient pairing of talent and opportunity" that characterized the non-networked job hunt. Ryan observes that "in a world without LinkedIn, it's the people who are already connected who get all the opportunities, and therefore get more connected." LinkedIn aims to help, he says, by making "everybody else a little bit more connected, so you can have those casual conversations that can easily lead to a great job and connections."

I hope you give some of these suggestions about LinkedIn a whirl. There's a reason it's become such a mainstay for so many people for so long. Ask any recruiter.

The Real-Time Network: Twitter
An experience you tailor to suit yourself.

Twitter is a constant, streaming swirl of in-real-time news, as well as serious, humorous, well-documented, off-the-cuff, outrageous, and/or provocative views on any topic imaginable. Many social-media-shy people think of Twitter as a bother: too much short-form noise about too many things that fly by in a flash. Some dislike the nasty comments and exchanges it can engender; others are hesitant about how and when to jump in. I understand these and many other concerns, but as someone drawn to unfolding news stories and information repositories of all kinds, I find Twitter invaluable for keeping up with the zeitgeist. Somewhat unexpectedly, it's also become a seamless way for me to connect with kindred spirits, many of whom I only know on Twitter. These are people I follow and get to know based on what they post, what I post, and how we respond to one another. Sometimes these are simply familiar online connections; sometimes you might know the other person in real life. You might not think Twitter could possibly help you find a job, but I urge you to keep an open mind (by the way, many recruiters and companies are very active on Twitter, and that's one of the reasons it can work well for professional connections). If you don't already use it, give it a try to explore avenues of interest, and see what comes.

What Twitter Is Best For

- **Staying current** with your interests
- **Gathering information** by reading tweets and asking questions
- **Feeling part** of communities you choose

Ever since Twitter began to take off beyond its early tech fan base, the core offering has remained: real-time short messages you can post in a few seconds. Today you can go "long" (up to 280 characters instead of the original 140), post a video, use umpteen emojis or GIFs, and so on. But the effect, and the benefit (for fans, anyway) hasn't strayed far from what David Carr, the late and inimitable *New York Times* media columnist, wrote in a 2010 story called "Why Twitter Will Endure." In it, he explained why he'd become a heavy user: "I'm in narrative on more things in a given moment than I ever thought possible, and instead of spending a half-hour surfing in search of illumination, I get a sense of the day's news and how people are reacting to it in the time that it takes to wait for coffee at Starbucks. Yes, I worry about my ability to think long thoughts—where was I, anyway?—but the tradeoff has been worth it."

My experience echoes that of Mr. Carr's, as does that of millions of people around the world today. It's very easy to tap in and find out what's happening right now: which topics are trending and why, how "Twitter" (meaning a slice of devotees attuned to one issue or another—politics Twitter or Black Twitter or dog Twitter, for example) is responding to the latest outrage or heartwarming story, who's got the best take on a news item, which soundbite (or video clip) will make you proud, irritated, or laugh.

Though Twitter (the company) encourages your active engagement, many people I know are strictly read-only. "I don't tweet," they tell me, "but it's where I get my news." I think that's fine, and perhaps even ideal, especially if your job demands being circumspect or you don't want to opine publicly or connect with others in front of everyone else. As for me, ever since I started using it in earnest nearly ten years ago, I've been a believer. Twitter is pretty great for learning from others, following ideas and discussions, and getting insights into new fields and opportunities. And yes, for making new contacts in real life—which is why it's one of the best ways to make and keep contacts you would not otherwise find.

For the purposes of this chapter, I'm writing about the standard account setup, which defaults to a public view of what you post.

Twitter Tip #1: Make Your Profile Count

Whether you are setting up your account for the first time or fine-tuning it, there are a few elements packed in the small space you get for your profile that you want to pay attention to. This is because the combination of your user name (the name with the @ in front of it) and the images you choose to represent and put at the top of your account make up your Twitter calling card, much as your LinkedIn Summary does for you on that service.

1. **Choose your Twitter handle wisely.** Your account name can be simply your name (upper or lower case; they work the same regardless of capitalization), or something entirely different. My own Twitter name, @kvox, is what I've used over the years for consulting. It turns out to also be great for Twitter, because it's short and not easily misspelled or mispronounced, as my last name often is.

2. **Decide what to mention or leave out.** Twitter profiles offer limited space. Some people are all business, but I notice

many others mix in personal interests with their vocation or current job. It's also a very nice touch to include a link to more information about you, whether that's your own site, your blog, Instagram account, or YouTube channel—steer visitors to the best representation you want out there. Go easy on the keywords and hashtags; as digital strategist Erin Blaskie has noted, "generic keywords help nobody."

3. **Consider your avatar carefully.** The small image that appears with your name on your Twitter home page also goes alongside every tweet you send. If your interest is in landing a job, you might want to go for credible with an easy-to-see headshot, and not a picture of you surfing a quarter mile out. A drawing or cartoon is fine, too; that's what I use for @kvox, because it resembles me (all thanks to Susan Kare). Your account image should represent you, too, to welcome conversations and exchanges.

Describing Yourself in Short Form

You can learn a lot about someone from their short-form description. As you see in this selection, humorous is fine, straightforward is fine, and combinations work, too.

- **@DrDonnaYates:** Archaeologist in a criminology department. I study artifact smuggling, art crime, heritage, culture. Arty stuff and related curiosities. Immigrant. Citizen.
- **@EricaJoy:** she/her/hers | Engineering @Patreon | Run from what's comfortable. Forget safety. Live where you fear to live. Destroy your reputation. Be notorious. —Rumi 🖤

- **@RadioKitty:** I write the words that wake you up. Radio maker. Nieman Fellow. Alum @MorningEdition @NPR. Teach @Georgetown. Emmy, The Civil War.
- **@GretchenAMcC:** Internet Linguist. Writing a book in defense of internet language @riverheadbooks. Former Resident Linguist @TheToast. Podcast @lingthusiasm (she/her).
- **@jemelehill:** Senior correspondent and columnist for The Undefeated. Born and raised by Detroit. Grew up at Michigan State. Fourth-worst Twitter account at ESPN.

You can change the elements of your account any time—the wording, the links, the images. Use the Twitter profile as your small canvas to represent your current obsessions or longtime passions. Every few months, take a look to see if it's time to freshen things up.

Twitter Tip #2: Curate Who You Follow, More Than Once

The real key to your Twitter experience is which accounts you choose to follow. From the minute you pick them, you'll see their posts cascading into your feed. A wonderfully quirky thing about Twitter is that sitting side by side, you and I would see a very different stream—our two feeds—and no two are the same. As a hard-core news reader, I follow a lot of reporters and publications. The result is that I constantly see a lot of chatter, commentary, and breaking news in real time.

But if you want to stay away from real-time events and instead devour pet videos, museum news, or everything sports—you can also find those tribes and hang out there. The same is true for causes, or academic research, or [fill in the blank]. This is foundational to Twitter: it's an experience you tailor to suit you.

If you're just starting out, here are a few ideas about who to follow:

- Twitter accounts of bloggers you like
- Through articles listing "top influencers" (or top specialists in X) on Twitter
- Suggested accounts Twitter offers when you add one to follow
- Look at accounts you enjoy following to see who they follow
- Your LinkedIn connections who have Twitter accounts

Twitter Tip #3: Use Your Hashtags

One of Twitter's most important features came about when an early user named Chris Messina suggested that typing a hashtag before a keyword or phrase could be a way for people to follow specific conversations, breaking news, and live events on the service. This practice took such firm hold that other platforms, including Instagram and LinkedIn, use it today. On Twitter you can create, or search for, events, conversations, and more through their unique signifiers.

Apart from large public happenings (#WorldSeries, #Grammys) and unfolding news stories (for example, #election or #hurricane), you'll want to use this feature to connect with others at conferences and meetings. Many such events create and actively encourage people to use a specific hashtag for the duration of the gathering. Whether you're attending live or following along online, you can comment, share photos, send questions, and find the speakers and others who are following the thread with you. It's a great way either to make a connection with someone of interest or to follow up with them after the event to pursue your conversation.

Twitter Tip #4. Keep and Subscribe to Twitter Lists

Twitter Lists are a handy way for you to group and track people by topic or interest. You can, for example, make a list of all the people you follow who comment on national news, another just for sports commentators, another one about books and authors—really any category you want to follow. Whenever you go to Twitter, you can view these tweets in a particular list or several without having to wade through the latest from every person you follow. In other words, you can customize your view fairly easily on any given day or session.

Lists can help you keep track of a lot of information thematically, rather than seeing sports scores right next to geopolitics in your feed. Think about how you want to organize your information: people you know in real life could be a list, or performers you like, nonprofit leaders, your favorite news outlets—really, anything that you want to track, including your professional interests. Lists are also very helpful for time-sensitive situations like natural disasters or accidents (wildfires, hurricanes, plane or train crashes), where people are tweeting from the scene.

- To **create lists** yourself, go to your profile page, and there you will see an option for Lists. Then, name the list so it will be clear to you later, and to visitors (e.g., "Women in Media"), and add the Twitter handles (account names) you want in that category. You can add or subtract names anytime, and when you want to see what's going on in the list you've created, just click on its name to see all of the latest posts from everyone in the group.
- To **discover lists** to subscribe to, look at the profiles of interesting accounts and click on their Lists (found on the right side, next to their Likes) to see which ones showing

under "Member Of" interest you. Click on the name to subscribe so you will see all the posts within. You can also use your favorite search engine to discover topical lists that others have rounded up.

Twitter Tip #5: Participate in Live Chats

Participating in a real-time conversation on Twitter can be valuable, fun, and lively. Typically, an organization like a news outlet or some kind of affiliated group conducts Twitter chats, usually on a set day and time. They will promote it beforehand, so that people following them know when to tune in. Twitter chats are great to learn from others, establish your expertise, and see who else you might connect with.

Chats have their own hashtag (for example, #AppChat about mobile app development, #DIYAnswers for home improvement, #SLChat for sports law, and so on). Some are long-running series that occur weekly or monthly. You can find a lot of chats to follow at https://www.tweetreports.com/twitter-chat-schedule/. One of my favorites, #ACESchat, is all about the finer points of editing, and their site thoughtfully features transcripts of past chats (https://aceseditors.org/resources/aceschat)—a nice resource for learning from others.

Twitter Tip #6: Express Yourself with Tweetstorms and Moments

Tweetstorms

A fairly recent Twitter phenomenon that some people (like me) love, and others hate (they'd rather read an article) is called a tweetstorm—a linked series of tweets on a particular topic that follow one right after the other, so you can read them sequentially in your feed. Many tweetstorms present an argument or background context on a current situation, based on the writer's personal experience or expertise.

This type of tweetstorm is like an outline of ideas or facts laid out one tweet at a time. Although Twitter hasn't yet given us a way to search specifically for tweetstorms or collect them in a category, you can save them for reading later by bookmarking the initial post that kicks off the series. I've read fascinating political treatises and personal stories, as well as useful how-to's on asking for a raise and the current state of startups in Berlin, as just a few examples of the topics people want to bring up.

The other type of tweetstorm is an unfolding story. One that lit up Twitter as I was writing this book was the tale of an office "lunch thief"—the quest to find out who had stolen a lunch from the office refrigerator. This dramatic saga actually led to news reports, not to mention many followers for the storyteller, Zak Toscani. It was hilarious, gripping, and inspired quite a few excellent jokes from those who followed it and many new followers. Twitter's ecosystem is large enough that such everyday tweetstorms can travel far because they can be swept along by a large wave of people.

If you'd like to try tweetstorming, keep these tips from *Lifehacker* handy: "Write your thread out in advance. Then check whether you delivered on the promise of your first tweets. Read it aloud; edit it thoroughly. Read it backwards. Trim it." Publishing a good tweetstorm is a wonderful way to show your style and get some notice.

Twitter Moments (https://twitter.com/i/moments)

Twitter Moments are collections of tweets that anyone can create and publish on Twitter. It's an interesting way to gather a variety of takes or reactions to a big story or a quirky one, or assemble a gallery (for example, make a Moment of red carpet fashion tweets, a championship win, a movie premiere). To see Moments on your mobile phone, use the search function (the magnifying glass icon), and scroll down to see new entries under "Today's Moments." On the web, click on Moments (with the lightning bolt icon) at the top of the page. You can also follow @TwitterMoments to see them all. Creating a Moment is an interesting way to express yourself and make a mark, since popular ones go viral.

Safety and Security

No credible discussion of Twitter and its features can overlook the issues the service has with people, often women, being trolled or publicly attacked on the platform. Though it pains me to say it, my former employer has been very slow to develop adequate tools and support to stop these practices as quickly and thoroughly as it should. I will note that some recently released features are helpful: you can report specific tweets or accounts directly through the app or the web; it's possible to mute, block, or report individuals; and it's also easy to report a specific tweet and tell Twitter directly why (you're not interested in it, it's spam, or it's "abusive or harmful"). If you see instances of harm or abuse in the making, I encourage you to follow and reach out to @TwitterSupport, and also visit the Twitter Help Center (help.twitter.com) to find useful articles on safety and more on reporting problems.

The Visual Network: **Instagram**
The way to see and say.

An image-sharing application that launched in 2010, Instagram has become the de facto home for visual artists and designers, performers and celebrities, and millions of creatively inclined people to share their art, their experiences, their travels, and a lot more photography and video stories. Since Facebook acquired Instagram in 2012, its popularity has soared, especially as Facebook has poured technical and creative support into growing the service across the world. Today Instagram has 800 million users worldwide. As with LinkedIn and Twitter, Instagram makes it easy to discover and follow people and accounts you're not directly connected to. That makes it particularly useful for some kinds of connections.

Unlike LinkedIn or Twitter, Instagram doesn't work well for sustained dialogue and deep written content. It's also not easy to get a comprehensive view of job openings or formally pursue a position, because it wasn't built for that. I'm including it here because of its huge popularity for people in creative fields, who make great use of it to showcase their work and connect with visually creative communities. In other words, it should be in your professional toolkit if it works for you.

What Instagram Is Best For

- **Self-expression** through photos and video
- **Seeing and sharing** what people enjoy
- **Discovering and connecting** with brands and creative people

Since photography and images are central to the service, Instagram is a wonderful avenue for visual self-expression, and you can create stories using image galleries or video in the application. Designers, photographers, fashion brands, celebrities, and performers all make great uses of it. I asked my contacts on Twitter and Facebook (most of whom are not designers, stylists, or fashionistas) how they use Instagram, especially for any professional connections. Just about everyone who responded told me it's strictly for fun—to see, share, and enjoy personal photos. Of course, Facebook didn't buy it just for fun; Instagram has become an important signifier of culture and style influencers that has drawn major advertisers and retailers. As video ads marketer Ryan Cochrane notes, "While someone's Twitter authority is typically measured by the number of followers held, and a Facebook page by its number of likes, Instagram authority is all about your most recent image—presenting the opportunity for anyone to be the 'go-to guy/girl' on any issue." So, if you're creatively inclined and want Instagram to be a featured part of your array of talents, focus on both your own posts and learn from the style makers you follow and connect with.

Instagram Tip #1: Bring Your A Game to Create

On Instagram, quality really counts. This isn't the place to post a shaky image from last night's concert. IG is about visual presentation, whether it's beautiful, dramatic, or clever. Take the time to compose photos and video carefully and get to know Instagram's filters and effects so you can make the most of them, such as the features that let you add captions, notes, and designs. As for video: practice, practice, practice. Whatever you post should tell a story people can grasp in a second.

Instagram Tip #2: Search Is Your Portal to It All

The best way to discover people, ideas, products, and new accounts is through the search function (the small magnifying glass icon at the bottom of the screen, next to Home). You'll see broad categories across the top for Instagram's biggest areas: Art, Style, Humor, Food, TV & Movies, Decor, Music, Travel, and so on. Another key aspect of the search function, handy for a professional focus, is the ability to search by Tags (also known as hashtags). Here you can try popular keywords (#jobs, #sales, #design) to see all the tagged posts for that word or phrase; for common words, there can be thousands. Click through on any image to learn more at an individual account. Quite a few companies also post visual "We Are Hiring" messages because they want to reach Instagrammers where they live. Look at #wearehiring or #nowhiring (and many variations you see when searching) for a vast array of results. Of course, the quality of what's been tagged varies wildly: search results here are very untamed, and you won't see informative summaries before going deeper. There's also a search function to locate accounts for people you know or want to follow. Instagram displays both real name and account name in results (e.g., Melinda Gates is @melindafrenchgates here).

Instagram Tip #3: Connect with People You Know

One of the key features of social networks is that you can connect your contact list to the service you're using to both invite friends to join you and to see who you know already using that service. Instagram operates as you would expect, and, of course, it's especially easy to connect with your Facebook friends. From your account settings screen, you can also see which non-Facebook connections use Instagram to follow them. Once you're following someone, you can send comments (which are public); if they follow you, you can also communicate 1:1 with direct (private) messages.

Instagram Tip #4: Connect with Brands and People You Discover

A never-ending source of inspiration and fun for millions of people, Instagram is an easy way to discover styles and trends. Browse to connect to those you love, get ideas about your own creativity, and show off your efforts.

Connecting with Creatives Through Instagram

Here are two stories I especially like about how people can make and keep professional connections through Instagram.

First, meet Alexandra Lange. She's a design critic and author who is always looking for new work by architects and designers. In an email interview, she told me that Instagram is a key tool for her to keep up with what's new. "There are so many biennials, design weeks, triennials—no one could go to them all. But Instagram, and now Instagram Stories, give a great sense of what the most striking displays are." And Alexandra benefits from constantly curating the accounts she follows. "Architects and designers like to know they are talking to someone who is on their wavelength, who thinks about the world visually. My own Instagram shows them that I know what's good, from what I choose to see when I travel, to snippets I notice in New York City, to how I frame architecture and objects," she explains. She also uses Instagram to chart trends: "An account that suddenly gets super popular, a long-dead architect or historic site that curators and designers are flocking to see—you can read between the images" to get a sense of what's garnering fresh attention.

Alexandra also takes advantage of Instagram when traveling. By sharing photos from a new place, she gets "the most engagement when people can tell I am on the ground somewhere—people tell me about additional places to visit, I get invitations to events and dinner, things like that." If you're wondering about the impact a well-tended social media presence can have, two years ago she was invited by the New Zealand Institute of Architects to visit, she says, "partly because of my social media (Instagram and Twitter). They wanted someone to show an American and international audience how great their contemporary architecture was. I wrote stories afterward, but the photos on social media had more reach." A key to developing such fruitful contacts is in part the awareness of you being active and informative on Instagram. (And, I'd add, on your other social accounts.) As Alexandra says, "There are lots of people who follow me on Instagram that probably never read my work, but they know I am out there spreading the word about what is worth visiting."

Next, here again is Ian Sanders, the business creativity consultant I wrote about in chapter 3. In an email exchange, he detailed Instagram's crossover value: "I love Instagram. That's one place I don't filter what I put up, I'm not trying to sell anything, I'm not thinking about my audience. On Instagram, I'm just being me." Ian adds that it's also a place for him to maintain important professional connections, citing this story: "Sonja and Sharon run a marketing agency in Bristol (UK). The three of us follow each other on Instagram. I saw them last week for a walk and talk. We hadn't seen each other for a year or two but having that connection on Instagram means we have a window into our lives. Without our connection on Instagram, I just wouldn't feel I know them so well. And our professional relationship wouldn't feel the same, it would lack that depth."

If you don't already use Instagram, I encourage you to download the app, create an account, and just poke around to get a feel for it. It may not be as central to your networking as other services, but it can still be a useful tool in your arsenal.

The Meta-Friend: Facebook
Connecting who you know, and sometimes who they know.

If you've just skipped to this section, you may be wondering why the biggest social network of all, Facebook, doesn't lead the list of tools you can use for connecting with others. It's obviously the behemoth in the room, but in some ways, it is the least applicable for our purposes. Although it's possible to use Facebook to develop meaningful connections with strangers, it wasn't designed for that specifically (as LinkedIn was, for example). Facebook was built for you to choose and connect with friends and family members within the Facebook environment, even though today you can actually have up to five thousand "friend" connections. (Note: nobody has five thousand actual real-life friends. Pew Research put the median number of Facebook friends for US adults at two hundred.) So, for the most part, Facebook isn't your first stop for making professional connections. But it does offer a few features that are valuable for this purpose.

If you're already active on Facebook, it's fine to take (reasonable) advantage of your circle to occasionally seek work advice, leads, and introductions. In my dozen years on the service, I've found the quality of information on professional topics varies wildly—it's not as focused as LinkedIn, or as public as Twitter, but sometimes having a few people weigh in who you know in real life, or by reputation, can be useful. If you are promoting a business or a product, you can create a Page, as it's known on Facebook. This is a public area anyone can discover through search, and on which you can manage and track engagement. You don't have to have a direct relationship with your Page followers (they are following the Page, not you personally). Alternatively, if you want to share updates from your personal timeline to more people than you're connected with, you can choose to let people follow you. That way anyone on Facebook (beyond your friends) can see your public updates in their News Feed.

As I write this in the spring of 2018, during prolonged scrutiny and a very public and ongoing conversation about how Facebook manages and tracks your personal information, be sure you are familiar with all of the newest settings for privacy and limiting the reach of your own information. If you want to hone your Facebook activity to job hunting and professional connections, the most useful feature may be Groups. You can find many of these by searching on the Groups link at the top of your Facebook home page.

The Flavors of Facebook Groups

- **Public:** Anyone can join a public group. The group details, including all the posts, are fully discoverable to anyone on Facebook. Some public groups have thousands of members.
- **Closed:** You must apply to join or be invited. The content of posts is only visible to members, though the group description and member list will appear in Facebook search results.
- **Secret:** You must be invited to join. Secret groups (and membership rosters) do not appear in search results.

Exploring Facebook for Groups to join requires a bit of investigating to find what suits you best. The Closed groups I'm in have thousands of members, too large for much active participation. I do read posts to get a sense of what the conversation is about, but don't comment much. I'm also in a couple of Secret groups, which have far fewer members, so it's easier to jump in with my thoughts. As with all discussion forums of any size and on any topic, you want to be thoughtful and focused when you do participate, as your words live on there.

Ground Rules for Group Participation

When it comes to career or industry-focused online discussion groups, it's worth understanding the rules of the group, especially if it's large and/or most members are not known to one another. A few suggestions for playing nicely:

- Remember that most groups don't operate in real time—it can take a while for people to respond. Don't dominate the conversation, answer every query, or put yourself in the center of every topic. People will get tired of hearing from you. That could be a turnoff to potential contacts, who might assume you're not collaborative, or are too self-involved.
- There are often rules in groups about confidentiality, particularly where personal topics like employment status and health matters can come into play. Treat others with respect and honor their needs to be circumspect.
- Aim to be useful. Groups aren't very interesting when there's a long line of "me too" and "I agree" messages that don't offer anything further. Add your story, link to a relevant article, make a specific suggestion that can help the other members.

The Best of the Rest

You may be a fan of other services that offer ways to connect with people even if their purpose isn't explicitly that. The business communications tool Slack comes to mind—even though it was built for company-wide communications, you can observe and learn and contribute with people you don't know well, as well as have private conversations on the side.

Similarly, you can connect with people you don't know via discussions and communities like Reddit and Quora. Depending on your interests and fondness for these services, go ahead and put them in your networking mix, provided you understand their context and usage before you plunge in. I do think LinkedIn, Twitter, and Instagram, with their broad presence and wide-range capabilities, are likely to be the most useful for nurturing your connections and interests.

With any or all of them in your toolkit, you can be taking part in the local and global conversations happening in your field(s) of interest. Whether you're thinking about your next career move, looking for inspiration, keeping up with your neighborhood and community, or simply looking for an old friend—at your own speed and on your own terms—you can find support and ideas and links to others.

It's a big, noisy world out there. I hope these tips help you to make the best use of your preferred platforms. They can be incalculably rich resources for networking, especially for those of us who hate the old ways of doing it.

No-Pressure Participation

The world's collective yearning for connection has . . . created a new status marker: the number of people who follow, like, or "friend" you.

— *"The Follower Factory,"*
New York Times

Whether you would like to broaden your circle of contacts, build a brain trust, or get into a new field or new job, you're missing out if you don't try your hand at making some simple online connections. With the right attitude and style, this no-pressure participation is your secret weapon for building your network.

Unless you've been living under a rock for a while, you've probably noticed that the word "content" has overtaken all the words we used to have for every type of self-expression, from writing to photos and video to movies and TV—even to the web itself. Now "content" is a catchall to describe all the stuff we see, make, and pass around online, the stuff we exclaim over and share with friends. I dislike the word because it makes all of this rich creative output we enjoy seem so clinical and of a piece.

Nevertheless, you can't avoid the word, and the universal idea behind it is that we humans love to watch, skim, read, and pass along what we love (or hate-watch). The good news about this endless stream of expression flying across our screens is that we can each react in our own ways, a lot or a little. However you participate, the most effective responses don't require you to call attention to yourself. You call the shots. And this ability to choose the content you create, share, and react to is your secret weapon to building your network.

It's taken me sixty-plus years to find the right balance between sharing my expertise and ideas without fearing self-promotion (that being anathema, of course, to any self-respecting introvert). The online world is one place where introverts have a big advantage: here we can quietly reveal ourselves to gain awareness and connections on our terms. (Sometimes I think the internet was created for those of us who loathe the idea of working a room.) If you're nimble at writing, at photography, at hot takes and clever asides, you can put yourself out there even as you stay behind the screen. You don't have to leave home till you're ready—and maybe not even then! Wonderfully successful people in all kinds of fields and endeavors work almost entirely online, from anywhere. How perfect for those of us who aren't crazy about crowds.

It's not only introverts who spend time online. As I write this in 2018, Pew Research reports that some 69 percent of all American adults use some kind of social media platform, a figure that's up across all demographic and age groups. And using these services, it's never been easier to register your appreciation, dislike, support, or pleasure about all kinds of causes and interests, around news, entertainment, and information. These services can also support your loose-touch habit—some of the best ways to socialize your thoughts and connect with others.

The Fine Art of Benevolent Lurking

In the overheated online and social media environment we're living in right now, overflowing as it is with breaking news and all kinds of disputatious political sinkholes, I understand the desire to lurk. The volume of chatter and opinion can seem so great that you don't want to get drawn in. Or maybe between work, family, and school, your life is packed enough without getting into any online fray.

But if you are strictly a "lurker"—someone who only reads what others say, and rarely or never comments or posts publicly—you're missing out on two things:

1. The ability to be found by anyone you'd like to connect with, since you have no obvious footprint (and if they can't find you, what's their motivation to connect?), and
2. A no-pressure way to express yourself, however quietly you'd like.

I know that online expression is not for everyone, especially when you're first wading in. Writer and editor Jess Zimmerman has used the wonderful phrase "benevolent lurking" to advise people considering the social plunge that "you will always contribute better, learn more, embarrass yourself less if you lurk for a while, if you watch which arguments play out and how and by whom." As she correctly notes, the online world can mirror real life: "In the offline world, 'social life' has a range of meanings, from constant chatter to quiet companionship. *It's important to remember that media can be social without being relentlessly extroverted.* (My emphasis.) Lurk for a while when you can."

Testing the Waters

If you're reluctant or new to revealing more personal bits about yourself online, your simplest expressions—clicking on Like or a heart, forwarding items without comment—is also you expressing yourself, developing your style and profile. These actions help you to see what your online expression style is. It takes very little effort to register your appreciation, support, dislike, amusement (and so on) using just a few words, or even simply an emoji or a meme. Since introverts in particular might be reluctant to jump in feet first, it's easy to test the waters this way. (It took me several years to warm up both on Twitter and Facebook. I did a *lot* of lurking first—and I still do in environments like Slack, where others have already formed communities I'm just joining.)

Even adding a short "this made my day" when you share or repost something you've enjoyed gives a sense of you and is preferable to no comment. People respond to people. People appreciate and want to become familiar with kindred spirits. Remember, too, that you always have time to deliberate on what you want to say. Think of it as adding a short postscript to your correspondence. For the reluctant, try to add a comment to support a cause you care about; chip in on a sports upset, weather madness, or pop culture figures in the news. These are fair game in a public conversation and don't need to land heavily or require too much revelation on your part.

TRY IT OUT: Study Your Self-Expressions

Many of us are already comfortable with our favorite services, with well-established patterns for what we say and do on each one. But what does your output say about you? Try this five-day exercise for a bit of self-discovery.

- **Five expressions per day.** This includes likes, hearts, emojis, or tweets forwarded with your comment. You must budget the five to last all day. What compels you to comment or share?

- Use your daily five on what strikes you as noteworthy or timely, and not simply as "duh!" or "like" endorsements. (Who doesn't love animal videos? But there will be more tomorrow.)
- Track your expressions every day for five days. You can, of course, skim and read or watch much more, but only react to five items.
- What does your collection of twenty-five expressions reveal? Did you spend it all on jokes, pets, or the political scene? How might someone characterize you by looking at what you've expressed and acted on? You might learn that you act most often on humor and pop culture, professional how-to's catch your eye, or you can't stop sharing athletic feats. This exercise is a good way to see yourself as others will and assess whether what you capture represents what you want to be out there. If someone takes a look at my (admittedly overactive) Twitter stream, the conclusion might be that I like my humor wry, follow US political commentary too closely, love dog photos, and am a nerd about digital culture. A fair assessment!

This may seem a trivial exercise, but it's important to understand how you come across in your social profiles, because that is often the most impression others will have of you. And that impression will draw them to want to connect with you or step away. It's yours to create.

What's Your Social Profile Style?

We're living in a time in which, as CareerBuilder reports, up to 70 percent of hiring managers review and factor in social media accounts to screen potential hires. How can you shape what your cumulative activity says about you?

There's not one-size-fits-all here; at least half the point of enjoying your social media presence is to express yourself. But—there's always a but, it seems—if your focus is on careers, job hunting, and professional development, you will want to pay some attention to what you're telling the world about yourself. In a *Harvard Business Review* study, business professors Ariane Ollier-Malaterre and Nancy P. Rothbard surveyed dozens of professionals to uncover four distinct strategies for crafting an online persona. First, they asked respondents to characterize their "most natural online behavior," from which the two derived four strategies for how to present your online self:

- *Audience*: Personal and professional accounts are separate; personal is very private.
- *Open*: Authenticity and transparency matter most; post whatever comes to mind.
- *Content*: Post only "carefully considered" content that projects professionalism.
- *Custom*: Tailor messages and categorize content for specific groups, audiences, lists.

What you decide to do, and how you showcase yourself, hugely depends on where you are in life, what your career is, and where you're aiming to get professionally. A performer has more latitude than an attorney. The key is what feels authentic and enjoyable for you, and what style serves your own goals. I know consultants who stick to business in what they post and share, and corporate employees who are incessant cutups.

Now that you have done the five-day test on your self-expression and absorbed the advice above about showcasing your best professional self online, let's take a look at the most familiar posting styles, and how to make good use of them for networking.

The Minimalist

These are people who pass along items (everything from hard news to evergreen stories to viral videos and memes) with little or no commentary and tend to be selective about what and how much they send out. This approach is handy for keeping up with your weak ties—to send out articles and items you think will be of interest.

Build connections by sharing useful information about a broad area of interest—for example, diversity and inclusion, the future of work, content branding, and so on.

The Commentator

These opinionated souls feel compelled to register their feelings about umpteen issues. No doubt you're familiar with the outraged commentator, but there are also well-wishers and jokers who want to say their piece to the virtual world about customer service (especially bad experiences), corporate responsibility, and other topics around business and society. If you're inclined to speak out, be strategic about what you share and say on those services where you have a professional standing.

Build connections by commenting on relevant business policies and practices you see with enough information to be useful.

The Uplifter

These are folks who are keen to provide a moment of relief by sharing good news, warmhearted stories, and plenty of "aww" moments. It's all positivity all the time and can easily blend with your professional self.

Build connections by sharing good news about corporations doing good, give a shout-out to scholarships, work-study programs, and effective community affairs projects.

What You Post, and Like, Counts!

If you wonder whether these self-expressions matter, I guarantee that people outside your circle *will* see them, for one of at least two reasons:

1. Recruiters, headhunters, and talent scouts for schools and jobs all over are always looking at people whose names they come across, or whose names are recommended through searches. They don't stop at LinkedIn, either. (And a word to the avoidant: according to the 2017 CareerBuilder study cited just above, recruiters are 57 percent less likely to interview a candidate they can't find online.)

2. If you want to be known as a go-to person, whether your field is cooking or artificial intelligence, even small public expressions can bolster that image or negate it. It's always good to pay attention to the signals you emit. Someone on the hunt for a speaker, consultant, or potential hire does not require you to showcase only one professional focus— but if you do intend to use social media for networking, your personal profile(s) should not appear discordant with your ambitions and desires. If you aspire to be known as an ace events planner, your online presence should at least support the idea that you can work under pressure and get things done. If your only online shares are about pub crawls, well . . .

Don't Dismiss Emojis

Widely available since Apple released its first set on the iPhone keyboard in 2008, emojis are a wonderful lightweight visual vocabulary you can use to add expression to what you share.

- **Creative punctuation.** Linguist Gretchen McCulloch, who writes about how the internet expands and changes language, describes emojis as "creative punctuation" that add color and a human touch to our expressions: "You'd feel weird having a conversation in a monotone with your hands tied behind your back, but that's kind of what it's like texting in plain vanilla Standard English."
- **When words aren't enough.** A recent *Fast Company* article noted that even in business settings, words aren't always enough: "Teams who are accustomed to working remotely won't always get a humorous reference or sarcasm, in large part because they only know each other digitally. So it's no wonder that emojis have become a common crutch to try to express our feelings."
- **A conversation closer.** Although emojis are usually the province of social media and texting, they're an efficient way to close out an email thread, with 👌 or 👍 (or another appropriately informal, but clearly understood, emoji).

This Is No Numbers Game

Early in 2018, a major *New York Times* feature story called "The Follower Factory" observed that "the world's collective yearning for connection has not only reshaped the Fortune 500 and upended the advertising industry but also created a new status marker: the number of people who follow, like or 'friend' you." When I talk about online participation, you might assume the next exhortation is about how you need to gain lots of followers. I'm not going to do that! The widespread adoption of social media has produced an ocean of how-to articles and a boatload of businesses intent on helping you "grow your followers" so that you can "be an influencer" with an active "engagement profile."

This intense focus on follower count has also led to a huge global industry for buying fake followers to pump up your numbers—something the *Times* article described as "a social global marketplace for social media fraud." Why do people do this? To boost their profiles, their name recognition, and often their business interests to increase their influence, and in many cases earn more money. The rise of bad bots—automated software designed to perform malicious tasks like stealing content or spamming online discussions—only adds to the fraud and confusion.

It's fine and great to become noticed, of course—but hear me out on this: never, ever buy followers. Between the fakery of it (and possible exposure for you when Twitter, Facebook, or Instagram remove fake accounts, as they periodically do) and the security risk if bad actors impersonate you, it's just not worth it. The quality of what you put out into the world matters far more than collecting an "adoring" virtual crowd. If what you are doing has value, and speaks to people, it will get noticed.

> If what you're doing speaks to people, it will get noticed.

A good example of someone who has nurtured notice and built up followers over time is Davida Lederle. She created The Healthy Maven, an online media business that draws readers, listeners, and viewers to a blog, podcast, Twitter (5,200 followers), Instagram (43,800), and YouTube channel (8,800). I went searching for influencers (she is one, by dint of her cross-media reach) in hopes of finding one who didn't seem obsessed about counting followers. She didn't disappoint: in a post called "The Slow Truth to Building an Authentic Brand Online" Lederle wrote, "I think it's easy to get caught up in wondering why one picture got more likes than another or why no one commented. That, my friends, is a big ole waste of time. . . . Just as you wouldn't fill your real life with fake, inauthentic relationships, don't overwhelm your online world with unrealistic pressure to perform for half-assed likes."

The Brand Is Still You

In a well-known 1997 essay, "The Brand Called You," business guru Tom Peters described the now-familiar idea about how we should each create a personal, individual brand for ourselves. Rereading the piece now is instructive, and even more relevant than it was twenty years ago. Though many of the examples that he wrote about then have evolved (you're much, much more likely to become known through your self-expression online than by writing a letter to the local paper), Peters was talking about the same thing I am now: making your skills, talents, and value known in ways that suit you. In that early essay, he said: "The good news—and it is largely good news—is that everyone has a chance to stand out. Everyone has a chance to learn, improve, and build up their skills."

The chances you have to stand out are not because you are buying followers or working up a sweat with hyper-"engagement." I can't put it better than Peters did back then: "Your network of friends, colleagues, clients, and customers is the most important marketing vehicle you've got; what they say about you and your contributions is what the market will ultimately gauge as the value of your brand. So, the big trick to building your brand is to find ways to nurture your network of colleagues—consciously."

Mohamed Zohny builds on Peters's ideas today. A social media leader for HP in Europe, he has written a helpful guide for creating an authentic online presence, and advises that the best approach is to "keep posting, keep learning, and keep improving." In other words, the good news for you, me, and introverts of all stripes is that other things matter more than metrics. I think the watchwords for a good social media experience are these:

- **Quality contacts.** Only you can decide which people you know, or know of, provide real quality. Their insights, their helpfulness, their responsiveness or offers to help, good humor—these are ways you want to "measure" your contacts. I know who is most likely to provide a thoughtful and nuanced answer; who will send me proof points and research; who is likely to respond with emoji. (I value everyone, but individual styles determine the value in the moment.) Those I don't consider to be high quality and wouldn't turn to are people who never respond or commiserate, who consistently object with "but" arguments, and who toss off thoughtless or snarky comments.

- **Artful engagement.** Here's a rule that should sound familiar: engage as you would want to be engaged with. Other people are putting themselves out there just as you are. Give them a hand, a hat tip, thanks, a few words of appreciation. If you're inspired to go deeper with commenting and sharing, do that, too, because that's likely to help you get a boost when you need it.

- **Judicious attention.** None of us can remember everything anyone is talking about that flies by on our screens, so take a moment to review the latest messages from someone you wish to contact before reaching out. That will save you from a too-cheery message when in fact your friend's dad just passed away. Or, in a less serious situation, paying attention lets you know that the person you'd like to introduce is traveling for several weeks.

If you've been following along, and doing the care and feeding of your network, you're placing your efforts precisely where they should be. The rest will take care of itself.

Email: (Still) the Killer App

Email is actually a tremendous, decentralized, open
platform . . . an exciting landscape of freedom amidst
the walled gardens of social networking and messaging services.

—*Alexis Madrigal*

We've talked about the benefits of cultivating a network, and
what's required to keep in loose touch. Now I'm going to
tell you about an easy, low-threshold way to cultivate, nurture, and
manage your connection to the many people that make up your
network, singly and in constantly mutable groups. Yes, it's email—
the modern convenience we love to hate. We complain endlessly
about having to wade through too many messages, getting too
much junk, we're never caught up, and on and on. What's more,
plenty of contemporary applications have emerged to supplant
it—text messaging, speech-to-text apps, social networks, team
collaboration tool Slack—but as *The Atlantic* writer Alexis Madrigal
has written, email remains "the cockroach of the Internet"—which
he means as a compliment.

Designed around the early open standards of the internet to be
used by all parties regardless of their online setup or service, email
standards have held up over many years. If you are, or can become,
a facile emailer, it's still the way to go for conveying information

privately or to a group. Even serial entrepreneur Elon Musk is a fan: "I do love email," he said in one interview. "Wherever possible I try to communicate asynchronously" (i.e., not in real time—one of email's best features).

This chapter isn't about specialized email organizers or achieving inbox zero. What I want to do here is show you how to think of email as a lightweight tool that helps you keep up with your network and meet new people, with a variety of examples. Email lets you cut through a lot of protocol and waiting time to meet people, respond, gather intelligence, debunk, get everyone on the same page.

When to Go Beyond Email

If you're already groaning about your inbox, let's start with a caveat: there are real-world limits to email as a tool. Sometimes it's better to get the job done via phone, a face-to-face meeting, or even by writing an old-fashioned letter. Here are some times when it's best to step away from the screen.

- When the email trail has gone cold on your important and time-sensitive request (make sure both things are true). Leaving a phone message or sending a text might unjam your message from the confines of the inbox.
- When there are a handful of people involved who need to make a decision, or have real-time updates (examples: *Do we need to meet in person? Where are we meeting? I'm running late.*). Depending on the specifics, texting can work, or a group scheduler like Doodle, when you've reached the limits of email efficiency.
- When it's clear email messages are simply volleying with no resolution in sight. Things aren't likely to be resolved this

way, so stop the thread by suggesting an in-person meeting or a call between parties.

- In the event of a crisis, a serious breach of etiquette, unintended personal affront, or life-changing event (marriage, birth, death, divorce) happening between you and someone you genuinely care about, be your most articulate self on paper and mail it. No emoticons allowed!

Best Uses of Email for Networking

Now let's look closely at how email excels at helping you make direct connections with other people. There's an art—and a bit of a formula—to each type of message: introductions, favors, and "Just FYI" (a.k.a. "thought you'd be interested").

Introductions

You know people worth meeting for specific reasons; you want to meet people for specific reasons. Therefore, we have an endless need for introductions, as a key to getting a fluid and functioning network. Sometimes you're the *asker* requesting a connection via a third person; sometimes you are the *askee*, the connector between two people. Even if we limit the protocol of introductions to business or professional interests, there's a virtual world of people to tap. And an email introduction is one of the most common ways people become connected.

When you're the askee, the one asked to make introductions, I encourage you to say yes much more than no, on the theory that you will need them yourself at some point. (There are times to say no, too, as we'll see.) Having an open mind for these requests is about more than building up good karma; it's about having a generous approach to others. Everyone needs favors; everyone needs a hand sometime. If you feel good about your web of relationships, why not share them? After all, it's likely you've relied on a casual connection that led to something new. Reflect on that generous act and carry it forward.

Here's a story about the serendipity of introductions, and how a slight gesture can have meaning. A year ago, I was having coffee with a woman I'll call Jan, whom I knew slightly—a business acquaintance. She'd recently left her communications role at a security company and wanted to update me on her job search. I found Jan sitting with her friend Margaret, who introduced herself as she got up to go. Margaret and I chatted briefly and traded business cards as she left. A year

> When you're asked to make introductions, always lean toward yes. You'll need them yourself at some point.

or more later, I remembered Margaret's specialty when a startup client asked me for leads, and I suggested her. Margaret got in touch with me, somewhat incredulous that our brief encounter had led to a potential business opportunity. To be honest I barely remembered the encounter, but I did remember Margaret's field and (after a brief check on LinkedIn) felt her experience matched the startup's need. The whole exchange was fairly effortless, and I'm glad I could spark an encounter between two people with related interests.

Wanting an introduction can be for any number of good and specific professional reasons: to learn more about a company, school, or profession; to hear about the new contact's experience working internationally or changing careers. Sometimes there's a time-sensitive aspect to an introduction request—for example, when the asker is interested in a posted job, and is doing some due diligence before applying or going in for interviews. I recently connected Sue, who was looking at a specific Google role, with

Robin, who unbeknownst to me had held that same role before being promoted. It was a fortuitous introduction that helped Sue prepare for the interview process. My only thought had been *Sue should meet Robin because Robin worked in that area.*

Sometimes a request for an introduction doesn't have a hard deadline—it's more for general information-gathering or to meet before next year's conference. The outcome here might be a call, a drink or meal, an email exchange—or it might lead to yet another introduction to someone closer to the question at hand. Whether a request is specific or general shouldn't really matter, though: it's okay to make them, and the answer most of the time should be a "yes" or maybe "how about this" (as in, "I would like to introduce you to someone who is more relevant to what you want to know").

Laying the Groundwork

Having vetted a request from your friend—and by the way, this should take no more than a single email or chat exchange—and assuming you *do* feel comfortable making a connection, let's look at how you might go about it.

First, let me emphasize two cardinal rules for making, or asking for, introductions:

1. Never send a "cold open" to both parties at the same time. It can be an unwelcome surprise.
2. Never pass along your contact's email for the asker to reach out on their own.

In the first instance, you risk annoying your contact for any number of reasons (the email address is private; they are constantly asked to do favors; they don't know you all that well; they are in the midst of deadlines, travel, personal crises, and so on). In the second instance, you might muff your one chance with someone you don't know simply because they don't like getting email requests from strangers. There was not enough setup. That's why you need the handoff from the person you know.

Now let's look more closely at an example of making the connection. Here's the initial note to see if your contact is open to an introduction.

Subject line: Hello and introductions

Hi _____ *(to the askee only)*,

It was great to see you last month, though too quickly, at XYZ conference. I wish we had more time to visit.

(OR)

It's been too long since we've caught up. I'd love to hear your latest news.

Aside from saying hello, I'm sending this note to ask if you would be open to speaking with my friend Wanda Livesalot. She is a _____ *(profession or role)* who would like to _____ *(meet, write to, call, hear from)* you because she is exploring _____ *(a new position, new companies, a new city, school)* and of course you came to mind immediately *(because of your knowledge/connections/specific ties)*. Wanda is _____ *(funny, unique, smart, clever, passionate, suited to your company . . .)* and I think you'd enjoy talking with her.

If you tell me it's okay to make introductions,

```
I'll follow up. But if you're not able to, or it comes
at a bad time, I understand. If that's the case, can
you suggest someone else for Wanda to speak with?
     Thanks in advance—I really appreciate it.
```

This note does several things:

- Reestablishes your connection to the askee with a bit of genuine small talk in the opener and signals that you either know, or want to know, what they're up to. The first focus is on your contact, not your request.
- Offers specific reasons and context for considering this introduction.
- Vouches for the person who is asking. (If you can't vouch, don't ask. Save yourself some reputational damage!)
- Makes clear that nothing happens without the askee's okay up front.
- Gives the recipient a face-saving chance to pass you along to someone else who might be better suited or more available.

I write a handful of notes like this every week, and I'm usually fortunate to get a yes in response. That's because people who know me know I've already vetted the person and the request, and that I aim to make only relevant and useful connections. Even so, sometimes I don't hear back. If I know the askee well enough to know that they are traveling or otherwise offline—but might be inclined to say yes—I will resend the original with a brief "I wonder if you missed seeing this, and thanks for considering" at the top. (Sometimes I get thanked for the extra nudge.) If I get an automated "out of office" message, I suggest to the asker that we try again later; if a return date is mentioned, I leave it up to the asker to remind me a day or two after that to send the follow-up.

Following Through on the Introduction

Once you've gotten the green light, here's an example of a note connecting the askee and asker.

> **Subject line:** Introducing Dale and Evan
> (*Easy for either one of them to find later.*)
> **cc:** Evan (*the asker*)
>
> Hello again, Dale (*the askee*)
>   Thank you kindly for agreeing to connect with Evan, cc:d here. As I mentioned, he's interested in pursuing an opening at BigCorp, and I told him you'd be the best resource. Also, Evan shares your interest in stand-up comedy, which should make your conversation even more enjoyable.
>   Thanks again, _____

Since you've already established contact with both parties, this is a shorter note. With luck, the two contacts will move you to bcc: (so that you don't have to follow their scheduling arrangements any further) and your work is done. The main thing you want to do, to the extent possible via email, is make each person feel comfortable about meeting or talking with someone they don't know. And, of course, it's important especially to thank the askee again, who is giving you (and Evan) the gift of his time and expertise.

By the way, I'm not the only one who pays close attention

to the protocol around email introductions. Roy Bahat, head of the Bloomberg Beta venture fund, has noticed an interesting geographical variance: "I am, repeatedly, surprised by the different work cultures on the East and West Coasts, and in technology versus other industries; it even extends to introductions. California intros, and intros in technology everywhere, tend to be shorter, less formal. New York intros, or intros in other industries (or nonprofits) tend to be more professional." Wherever you are, the same rules for email and introductions apply; it's your style that will vary based on the characters in your scene.

Favors

Favors often require more than simply passing one person along to another with a brief exchange. They are more specific, often have a deadline, and maybe even some follow-up by you, if you're doing the connecting. Favors can be about any number of things, like:

- Asking for an interview (media, research, informational)
- Seeking a recommendation for school or job
- Supporting a nonprofit cause (attending an event, donating, spreading the word)
- Endorsing the asker (e.g., nominating or voting for speakers, events, or boards)
- Suggesting or recommending a contact for client business or an exclusive event

Let's look at both sides of the "favors" scenario, starting with those times when you're granting a favor. When someone reaches out asking you to help with anything like the items above, understand that you need to assess a few things right away: the appropriateness of the request; you being the one to carry it out; your relationship to the askee; whether the timing is right. You doing a favor depends a lot on how comfortable you feel linking two people for a purpose that goes beyond you. Here again, the *asker* is whomever has the need and wants you to help; the *askee* is the contact you think can help. Use this checklist to consider which favors you want to act on.

- **How well you know the askee.** If you're cowed by the thought of asking, maybe the answer is "not well enough," and you should suggest another route. Recently I caught up with a former colleague who wanted to meet a well-established venture capitalist I know only slightly. I told my friend he'd have better luck asking another mutual acquaintance, who knows the VC much better than I do.
- **Understand what the asker wants.** You should have enough intel and context to gauge whether this is a reasonable request you don't mind doing. If the askee wants to talk about opportunities in a certain field, or for a specific job, be sure to get enough context so the request goes beyond "you two should meet" (that can be irritating to the recipient). For example, explain that *"Joe is looking for his next opportunity, and he's intrigued by how your company handles customer service"* or *"Monique told me how much she enjoyed your recent report on digital marketing for local business, and she would like to discuss it further with you for her master's thesis."*
- **Make sure the request is reasonably open-ended.** Requiring a tight turn-around out of the blue isn't a good way to endear yourself to someone you're asking a favor of. Make

sure there's a reasonable amount of time, or that it's an evergreen request, so you're not seen as being demanding (or rude).

When You Need a Favor

When you're seeking help, it's vital that you understand that it can take time and effort on someone else's part. Your first step in this scenario is to think through what you're asking. Here's a short checklist:

- Does your connector need to do any research to forward your request—about your background or the situation at hand—in order to make the ask?
- Do they have everything they need from you in an organized fashion (e.g., a PDF or clearly identified link that is easy to pass along without extra effort)?
- Have you explained the context of the request entirely to your contact so that no one is caught off guard by facts that differ or other people also stepping up to help you? (It's no fun to find out that you've sent identical requests to five people without telling them. You risk losing a lot of cred by less than full disclosure when seeking a favor.)

Asking a favor via email is similar to handling an introduction, in that you want a thorough story. So, get all the details to forward to your contact (including the all-important deadline); put in a word about why you think this is a worthy request; and make it clear that you won't move ahead without hearing back. This last point is even more important in that a specific action rests on it, and without their okay, the asker needs to move along to other sources.

Recently a good friend asked me to connect her to someone known in his field that she thought might be able to provide a back-cover blurb for her new book. Such a task carries several obligations: there's a hard deadline, the blurber is agreeing to read (or at least skim) the book and say something positive about it publicly. It's not a small favor, but it can be a meaningful one for both parties. I passed along all the book details and emphasized why I thought my contact would be a good reader/blurber. He readily accepted. After connecting him to my friend, my work was done. I hope he reads and enjoys the book, and I look forward to what he says about it if he does.

Here's how a note for a favor might go. I sent this one to a professional contact I see every few years; she was going to speak at a workshop that a friend of mine was planning to attend.

Subject: Favor when you're in Washington on March 23 (*The subject line indicates a time-specific request from you.*)

Helen,

I hope you are traveling only as much as you want these days—though I'm certain that's still a lot!

As for me, I am now consulting, too. I love keeping my own schedule and love the variety of projects. I bet you can relate.

I'm writing because a good friend and former colleague, Rebecca Jepson, would like to meet you when you speak at the Press Club in Washington on March 23.

```
     After finishing an MA in analytics, she is now
creating a new measurements program across her team,
about 250 people globally.
     May I introduce you ahead of time, so you might chat
for a few minutes after your talk? She's delightful.
     Thanks in advance, _____
```

As you see, the note is to the point but includes enough information that the recipient can quickly decide what to do. Did you catch the main elements? This is what you need to cover.

- Open by indicating your awareness of her schedule and professional standing.
- Briefly mention what you're up to and make it relevant.
- Remind busy people specifically where and when you need the favor, and any deadline.
- Give brief, relevant context about who needs the favor.
- Provide specifics of the actual favor, with your added endorsement of the person needing it.
- Add or repeat your appreciation when signing off.

Now let's move into the realm of keeping in loose touch via email with no special agenda.

Just FYI (a.k.a. "Thought You'd Be Interested")

This category of email can serve a number of purposes: you use it to keep in loose touch, reconnect with someone, follow up with a new acquaintance. The nice thing about a "Just FYI" message is that there's no real obligation involved on either side, and you are top of mind for a moment with the recipient (which helps solidify your ongoing relationship).

TRY IT OUT: 5 Easy "Just FYI" Notes

Apart from the link or attachment, your message is essentially along these lines: *this confirms what we talked about; I wonder what your reaction is; reading this reminds me of you.*

1. **Send a relevant article to someone who interviewed you for a job you didn't get.** Even though it didn't work out, you liked that person you met, and want to stay in touch. Show that you're a good sport and still attentive to the company and industry. (Just don't revisit the job interview.)
2. **Say hello to someone you met at a conference last year** with the just-published agenda for this year's event.
3. **Share interesting news about your old company with a former colleague.** Former coworkers are sometimes the best weak ties—you may not have known them well, but there's a feeling of kinship. A simple note asking what they're up to along with a story can keep the connection going, or even strengthen it.
4. **Show you're paying attention to your weak ties** by sending them items (news, event, commentary) related to their interests. For someone you don't know well, this will give a moment of delight and appreciation. What you send is based on what you know: are they presenting at a conference, doing research, passionate about a project, focused on an emerging trend?
5. **Reinforce a connection you just made** by following up with relevant information. If you just met someone and talked about mobile phone usage, send the news story you spotted on this with a brief note ("This made me think of our conversation").

Whatever you send conveys your awareness (or respect, or fondness) for the recipient. It is likely to engender a good feeling and might surprise you by leading to reciprocation ("I've been meaning to get in touch, too")—but that's not why you're doing it. Here's an example of a no-obligation "Just FYI" note I sent recently to a friendly professional contact in the field of autonomous cars. I thought of him after seeing a tweet about an upcoming workshop on that topic.

> **Subject:** Do you know about this conference?
> *(The subject line should tease the information you're sending instead of being a generic "hi".)*
>
> Hi Jimmie,
>   I hope you're faring well in these fun times.
>   Just ran across this [link] and thought of you.
>   Happy Monday,
>   Karen

Even this short note accomplishes quite a lot:

- "Fun times" is a reference to the surge of news about autonomous cars, which is sometimes wacky, negative, or inaccurate. This mention conveys a bit of sympathy about what Jimmie deals with.
- You don't have to explain a lot if you include an informative link. In this case, it was the home page for an upcoming workshop for policymakers working on issues surrounding self-driving vehicles. Note that it was the site for the event itself, not a news story about the event—the former is more useful and direct.
- Even the closing line, "Happy Monday," says "I'm not looking for anything from you. Do what you like with this information."

Even though I wasn't looking for a response, Jimmie wrote back in a few minutes to say that he had just registered for the event. I love the fact that I came upon the right thing for him, and I get a lot of satisfaction out of such small moments. This took no more than two minutes and didn't require any real effort on my part or his.

Sometimes "Just FYI" can be a bit more personal—an inside joke, a current meme making the rounds, relevant sports victories or defeats, a glowing (or scathing) review of a series you've both binge-watched, a political gaffe gone viral (where you share the same outlook, of course). Here the brief message might be along the lines of "I just had to send you this," or "Do you believe it!? Hope you're well."

Such messages matter in hard times, too. If your contact has suffered a corporate downturn or the industry is on the ropes, a short note saying, "I'm thinking of you" and a link to a positive story or column on the topic might help, along with a general "please let me know how I can help" works. The main point is to convey some kind of kinship in the moment with no expectation of further action. Whatever the tenor of a "Just FYI" message, not much language is required. But you do need to be sure-footed about the emotional tone of what you send. The better you know the person, the more latitude you have to be casual or irreverent. The intent is the same, though, whether you're close or not.

Despite the many gripes we have about it (and certainty by some that it will soon be replaced), email continues to have a unique value. But as with a lot of technologies, our unhappiness with it is mostly not the fault of the tool, but how we humans misuse it. I hope some of what you read here helps you get more from one of the most valuable stand-alone tools we have for direct communication.

PART THREE

GETTING REAL

A good improviser is someone who is awake, not
entirely self-focused, and moved by a desire to do
something useful and give something back and who
acts upon this impulse.

—*Patricia Ryan Madson*

The Real World Beckons

The easiest thing is to react. The second easiest thing
is to respond. But the hardest thing is to initiate.
—*Seth Godin*

All the things we can (and should) do online are efficient, effective, and even fun—but at some point, there are obligations
we have to deal with out in the world, with other people. For
one thing, many of us are required to participate in work-related
meetings and social obligations with our team or company. And
there's always an abundance of workshops, presentations, and
mixers that can be beneficial for your career, current or future,
however unpleasant the idea of actually going may seem.

This chapter is all about navigating the real world without
losing your mind or your soul. We'll walk through how you can
deal with optional events and meetings, as well as those you've got
to do in order to be a "team player" (to the corporate-minded, this
is the Valhalla of winning characteristics). Believe me, I've done
my share of grimacing at the idea of "enforced fun" at a team
offsite or at the notion of small talk at an industry event. And
yet, when I do make the effort, I'm often rewarded well beyond
my (admittedly low) expectations.

When Showing Up Is Not a Choice

Let's talk first about what you mostly can't avoid: obligatory work events. If even contemplating such an event brings on deep irritation, one physical boost you can give yourself is to wear clothes you feel comfortable and confident in. Or, this command performance may be a good reason to buy something new—clothing, shoes, jewelry—that will help you feel your best.

Now to the obligations.

Team or Company Offsites

If you've ever worked at a sizable organization with several teams or offices, you're probably familiar with the "offsite" (quotes added here because they are often, in fact, "on-site"—in the office—though the group gathers away from their usual workspace). When I was on the Google communications team some years ago, we had grown to about three hundred people, working in many countries. At that size, we held an all-team confab once a year at HQ in Mountain View, California. The offsite had an elaborate week-long schedule featuring many speakers and breakout sessions, plus social time with dozens of teammates in the evenings. The point of this socializing was to create bonds between us that would bolster our regular routine of video calls and email. And in fact, this time together did result in a much-improved ability to get things done. As a reluctant networker, my first impulse is to bemoan this demand on my time, but these sorts of intermittent real-world connections can be worthwhile. Years later, I'm still friendly with quite a few of my far-flung Google colleagues.

Workday Obligations

When it comes to team lunches or group outings, company politics and optics make it hard to skip them. If you do, you risk that infamous "not a team player" label. So, go—any genuine conversation is a bonus—and make a point of following up individually with people afterward for coffee or walk-and-talk meetings. One on one, some colleagues can be genuinely helpful for understanding dynamics between teams; they might have good information about a current project; they may have an inspiring career story to tell you.

Make such dates a regular habit: whose role, or team, would you like to know more about? Who seems interesting to you (regardless of role or team)? These are the people to get to know and can become part of your network. I learned this very early at Google, where my projects led me to scores of people and teams around the company. Years later, I've maintained friendships and professional connections with a lot of great people through those sometimes brief interactions.

> Follow up individually for coffee or walk-and-talk meetings. One on one, some colleagues can be genuinely helpful.

The Dreaded Company Party

When I first pitched this book to publishers, my proposal noted that in recent years I'd skipped corporate holiday parties—they had gotten to be too big, packed with too many people I didn't know (even people I had never seen before, and I don't mean spouses). This mention got a lot of notice in our meetings: apparently very few people enjoy going to these well-intentioned but often mandatory parties.

Once Google's holiday parties had grown to thousands of employees-plus-ones, the chance I'd even run into anyone I knew grew slim. There are, of course, more disincentives for such mega-events: the chance for any kind of meaningful exchange is low, and the likelihood of an open bar. Since it's easier to mingle with a glass in hand than with a plate, many people end up having too much liquor and too little food. Another reason to stay home: as a singleton, I don't want to have to ask a friend to endure the onslaught of forgettable introductions and work-related banter. (If you have a friend with whom you can trade the favor of going to these work-party events, and you're in the right frame of mind for it, that's a way to go, too.) But you get my point: honestly, I'd rather walk the dog!

If you're at a smaller organization, your parties might be (slightly) more fun. You're likely to know most of the people in the room, and with luck you'll have genuine camaraderie and social time with your team. Good for you—but remember, it's still work. As a recent *Vice* story put it, " 'Work parties are ostensibly social events that takes place with those you work with . . . for which you are not being paid to attend, because it's optional. . . . Except it's not really optional because of the office politics that bubble to the surface whenever the lines between 'work' and 'not work' get blurred."

In these scenarios, politicking and career preening are to be expected; there's a "see and be seen" aspect you can't avoid. Assuming you dread going, my advice is to either go early, circle the room twice—making sure you're seen by whomever "needs" to see you—and then leave; or go later, after you've had a nice dinner elsewhere. Make that same brief circuit, and exit.

Bottom line: Don't waste time doing something you absolutely dread, and from which you won't benefit much for the effort. But if you *are* obligated, keep your appearance brief. You can honestly say you went and get points for that.

Alison Green, who offers great advice about all kinds of work issues at her site Ask A Manager, says much the same: "Show up for an hour, put in an appearance, walk past your boss a couple of times so they see you're there, then go home. If you have kids, they're a good excuse."

When Showing Up Is Optional

Beyond required employee meetings, there are times when you should attend conferences or workshops. At least part of the point of these confabs is to meet people, whether to broaden your knowledge for your current job or to connect with others about your future options. Your assignment is to make these gatherings as useful as possible *for you* in the hubbub of people who are badge-reading and looking beyond you to see who's coming. (We've all been there.)

Surviving the Conference Circuit

Whether you're going to a specific work-related event or a broader industry or skill-building meeting, remember: you are not required to work the room or meet all the people in it. There's no need to transform into an automaton. Instead, be strategic about two or three goals you want to achieve from your time in the scrum and pursue those: learn a new thing, zero in on a handful of people or companies you want to meet, declare victory, and go home.

Let's say you go to a conference or trade show that lasts a couple of days. Before you head into the fray, study the schedule. Pick the sessions that are genuinely most interesting to you. If possible, some of these will align with the time of day when you most feel up for being in a crowd. As a morning person, my standard MO is pump myself up for the first part of the day, because I know I'll flag later. I always go early enough for coffee and walking-around time, up to an hour before sessions begin. Some people I know prefer to come just before the lunch break and eye the crowd to find promising tablemates for the midday speaker. Or you might want to stop in for the final session and stay for thirty minutes of the cocktail reception that follows. Whichever way you work it, block out at least an hour on the premises for mingling—enough time to size up the situation and perhaps connect briefly with one or two people.

As for the conference schedule itself, you can also make light-weight connections as you wait for the keynote or participate in a breakout session. Most people in conference mode are primed for a brief chat you can close by saying, "I'd like to follow up—may I have your card?" (Sans cards, you might beam your coordinates into each other's conference app, ask to connect on LinkedIn—however it works for you.) If people are wearing badges or name tags, look available to talk instead of studying your phone—make eye contact.

In a 2017 essay memorably titled "How This Anxious Introvert Handles Large Events," venture capitalist Hunter Walk lists several useful gambits for making the crowd scene tolerable, especially if it goes on for more than half a day or so. Among other things, he suggests taking time-outs to recharge—a circuit around the block, a solo drink—something to help you renew before heading back in. Another idea: stepping away with one person. He writes, "I'm a big fan of catching up over a 1:1 walk, even offsite from the event. I find this technique especially good at evening events where instead of a loud noisy drinking circle, I'll find someone

I wanted to spend time with and we'll . . . just sit and chat for 20-30 minutes before releasing back into the frenzy."

TRY IT OUT: Striking Up a Conversation at Events

Conferences are a low-stakes place for a little chitchat. It's not only acceptable, but it can be very efficient while you're at the coffee bar or waiting for the speakers to begin. During breaks I'll circulate, making it a point to seem unhurried and open to others, phone at my side and not in front of my face. Standing in line to get in or to get a snack is a great place to say hello; with luck, see their affiliation (if the badges are readable); and have a quick exchange. And if you establish even a bit of a connection before running out of time, here's where a business card is handy for following up. (There's more on using business cards later in this chapter.) Here are some openers:

- **"How long have you been with [company]?"** is a decent way to start, ideally followed by a general compliment: "That's a crazy/fascinating/stable space to be these days."
- **"What brings you here?" or "How are you liking the conference so far?"** are old reliables if identification is elusive. It's better to frame an open-ended rather than a yes/no question, like "Are you enjoying the conference?".
- **Keep your personal elevator pitch handy.** But if you're not ready to go into your short spiel about your current or future professional life yet, it's fine to get the other person to talk.

Small and Informal Meetups

These can take different forms: you want to stay in touch with people from the continuing education course you just finished; an employee diversity group wants to meet employees from other companies; a work team wants to explore doing a charitable project outside the office. If you're motivated, you shouldn't have trouble sticking with it. If you drag your feet, that's a sign that you're not getting the value out of it that you need, or the timing isn't right for you. No harm, no foul.

Continuous Learning

There are loads of optional events that help you in the long run: to learn about a field you want to get into or a company you're interested in. Sometimes author talks can provide an overview about a currently hot topic (digital health care, say, or financial security) to broaden your understanding. A career coach I know recommends going to one every quarter, especially if you are a consultant instead of a salaried employee. They keep you in circulation and up to date on what's new.

As I write elsewhere in this book, being open and having a sense of curiosity about events that help you professionally are generally good things. To gauge whether or not to attend a career-enhancing (but optional) event is a must-go or skippable, ask yourself these questions:

- Will people I like be there? (At a minimum, I can hang out with them and get through the evening.)
- Is there a speaker I want to hear, or a topic I'm genuinely interested in? In Silicon Valley, I could fill the week with sessions on "the future of mobile payments" or "robots vs

jobs," so a speaker who has an interesting take on the topic, or a knowledgeable interviewer, can make the difference.

- Is it in an interesting place? Recently I went to a press event on the issue of global trust because the subject interested me, and also because I was curious to see the new event space where it was held.

- Does it help me professionally? Because I work with all kinds of businesses, I need to keep up with the latest industry thinking on several topics. To get consulting work with artificial intelligence companies, it benefits me to be conversant with the issues in that field, so I look for low-threshold events I can learn from.

In a word, go. Or go sometimes. It's good to get out into the fresh air.

Business Cards Can (Still) Be Useful

Back in the day, a printed business card was something people at a certain level received at a new job, and people who didn't aspired to have them. But for many of us, the business card era is passing. It's a rare person today who physically files them for ongoing reference, which every executive assistant used to do as a matter of course. You and I already have our contacts on our phones, and that's the most efficient way to store them. (Just remember to update them, which is imperative for staying in touch.)

Despite their decline, I'm here to praise the printed business card, at least for some uses. It's a handy little souvenir that reminds you to follow up with people you meet in person, especially during time-limited encounters at professional events. You may not get far enough in your brief encounter to establish the reasons to connect, so proffering a small card with a handwritten note is useful. (Even if they don't have a card, get their email address so you can follow up. Don't expect them to.)

TRY IT OUT: Following Up After an Event

Whether you collect paper business cards, send contact details via your phone, or rely on a scribbled note, follow up soon after you've met a new person. Within a few days, you should send a note to:

- thank them for the connection
- remind them of why you want to connect
- include relevant information (link to article, resume, LinkedIn profile, offer to make introductions, and so on)
- invite a response at their leisure (don't push unless you've established in person that you have a deadline, and they've more or less agreed to help)

The other reason a printed card can work goes back to Tom Peters's "The Brand Called You" idea I discuss in chapter 7. In an era where artisanal brands and personal styles are flourishing, it's possible to make good use of cards if you're in a creative field, want to stand out, or conduct face-to-face business. And if you're a consultant or contractor, or are trying to break into a new field, a card can signal your aspirations to others in clever ways.

When I left Twitter to start my own consulting business, I thought a lot about what I wanted to say about myself. I knew I wanted a printed card because it can serve as a kind of memento of an encounter. (Collect them long enough, and you have your own time capsule.) To be most utilitarian about what to say, I could describe myself on a new card as being a Writer and Editor—that would have done the basic job. But I wanted to suggest that I can offer greater value. After all, decades of writing and editing has also bolstered and built other skills. So, in making a new card, I settled on three ideas:

- **Communicator:** An umbrella term to cover my interest in clear communication, whether through writing, speaking, or strategy.
- **Curator:** I have a lifelong habit of finding and collecting all kinds of information for people that I think they'll enjoy or find useful. (And as I've noted, a great skill for keeping in loose touch.)
- **Reality checker:** This is a nod to many years of corporate life. I know how organizations work, how people behave inside them, how to read the office landscape and the outside world on behalf of a company.

Apart from those three lines/four words, and a delightful pixelated image I was lucky to get as a gift from my friend, the celebrated icon designer Susan Kare, the only things on the front of the card are my email address, phone number, and a short link to my About. me page. (About.me is a service that offers a single page on which you can include a paragraph's worth of copy and links to whichever services people can use to find out more, or to contact you—a handy summary site.) And that's it. For fun, I chose to add inspirational quotes on the back—a bonus bit of whimsy for the recipient curious enough to turn the card over. I ordered my cards in four colors, so each batch features a different quote, each of which reflects a thought that resonates for me. These are the quotes I picked:

The art of life is not controlling what happens to us, but using what happens to us. —*Gloria Steinem*

Specialization is for insects. —*Robert Heinlein*

The trick is to be grateful and hope the caper doesn't end soon. —*David Carr*

Happiness is not a goal; it is a byproduct. —*Eleanor Roosevelt*

If you're working for yourself or thinking about it, you may want to consider a printed card for the same reasons I did: to pique interest, have some fun with a traditional format, and give people you hand it to a more than usual reason to follow up. A card doesn't do all the work, but with the right intent, it can help open doors and help someone remember you. There's no shortage of services and design ideas for creating cards, so if you're going to go that route, consult someone with a good eye to help you capture the most important aspects of your field and work that you can convey in a small space. It's key that you have at least two of these: email address, account names for wherever people can find you, the URL of your own site or info page.

When I get home from a conference or another event, I add the latest few cards to a small pile I keep by my laptop, to remind myself to follow up. (Eventually, the contacts either make it into LinkedIn or my contact database, or they don't, and I recycle.) As for printing, don't overdo it. On-demand printing services make it easy to order a small number that can last a long time.

A final word about the business of business cards: if you have a job that comes with a standard business card, but you have a side hustle or want to explore other possibilities, either make your own card to give out when appropriate, or if you're in a profes-sional setting like a conference, hand over the "official" card, but add your personal email address (or LinkedIn contact) to make a connection. I'm always surprised when people who want my help to find their next gig give me their current work email. Always use a personal account when you're prospecting. Keep your quest off of your employer's servers!

Whether your job requires it, or your job search makes it neces-sary, showing up in person is just a fact of almost everyone's work life. You may never actually enjoy or look forward to required professional encounters, but perhaps I've convinced you that they are eminently survivable. And if my experience is any indication, there are strategies to manage them so that maybe they turn out not awful at all, and even rewarding.

The Art of Small Talk

> When you talk with strangers, you make beautiful
> and surprising interruptions in the expected narrative
> of your daily life. You shift perspective. You form
> momentary, meaningful connections.
>
> —*Kio Stark*

A lot of people, including those of us who are networking skeptics, deride small talk for good reason: it can be vapid, generic, and is rarely personal. Chitchat obliterates quiet space and is often too trite to bear ("Hot/cold enough for you?" "Traffic is terrible," "Thank God, it's Friday!" and so on, *ad infinitum*). It usually doesn't account for your state of mind or current mood, and it often seems as if the habitual chatterer is nervous, egotistical, or is otherwise missing a social skill. When I posed the question, "What do you hate about networking?" on Twitter and Facebook, one of the most consistent replies was about the irritating dialogue people associate with it: "awkward," "forced," "canned," "inauthentic."

I've come by my long-standing dislike of small talk thanks to my dad's family: three generations of South Dakotans of Norwegian heritage, which is to say nary a chatterbox in the bunch. So when I find myself in Small Talk City, I quickly look for the exit.

However, much to my surprise, I've recently come around a bit. I see that small talk *can* serve a purpose, even for introverts and others who are small talk avoidant. Judiciously deployed, it can serve to lessen tension or navigate a peculiar social moment; it can help us to transition in or out of a room; it can send a momentary signal of friendliness or peace. I've also learned that we're not the only mammals who vocalize to establish bonds. As a Princeton-led study on lemur vocalization (yes, lemurs—those googly-eyed mammals from Madagascar) discovered, for them, "Talking is a social lubricant, not necessarily done to convey information, but to establish familiarity." The study concluded that the sounds they make "are equivalent to the chitchat that we do," and cannily observed that "most of the time we have conversations and forget them when we're done because they're performing a purely social function." So true, and now we know lemurs are like us.

> For lemurs and humans both, "Talking is a social lubricant, not necessarily done to convey information, but to establish familiarity."

Getting Comfortable Making Small Talk

Even though I dislike mindless chatter, a brief exchange in passing gives me a nourishing moment of shared humanity. I'm talking here about a little back-and-forth with a fellow dog walker, corner store clerk, sister elevator inhabitant, the office cleaner or security guard. To make note of the cute dog, the bad weather or bad traffic, sports victory, or upcoming holiday provides a sense of camaraderie and connectedness that I think even introverts desire. (And a possible bonus if the small-talkee opens up with a tantalizing story or news you didn't know.)

In a 2016 *Slate* essay, writer Ruth Graham defended small talk as a "crucial social lubricant," predicting that it "will always be with us, because it's the solid ground of shared culture. The more divided a people—culturally, politically, economically—the fewer conversational topics we can share. The more productivity-obsessed, the less time for old-fashioned pleasures. And that means small talk is no small thing at all."

Safe, Friendly Small Talk Gambits

Here's the good news about most small talk: it doesn't last long. Even a mindless exchange is over before you know it. And one characteristic that can help you get through these encounters: They're largely observational, and shared, rather than investigative or personal. Typically, they're based on something you both see or are likely to experience, such as:

- slowness (elevators, crowds, lines)
- weather-related (too cold, too hot, rainy, snowy, humid)
- traffic (bad, unexpectedly good, constant)
- local sports (wins, losses, celebrations, traffic)
- weekends and holidays (anticipation for what's coming up, sorrow about what's ending)

Small Talk at Work

Since so much of our lives is spent around people we wouldn't otherwise know, let's look at how small talk functions in that setting. For one thing, *listening* to office small talk—if you work in an open plan office, this is practically unavoidable—can give you knowledge that helps your understanding of others, and that understanding is invaluable for being able to get things done, to collaborate, and to have a good sense of group dynamics. I once worked on a project with a guy from a different discipline who, I had learned by listening to his office chatter, was forever negative. He was critical by nature of the smallest thing to the biggest idea. By picking up on his constant put-downs, I was able to win him over by out-naysaying him—recognizing (but not agreeing with) all of his complaints before he could raise them. That made him feel listened-to, which cleared the way to actually getting something done. As for the artful deployment of *making* small talk, it can help coworkers you don't know feel more at ease—a social lubricant, in Ruth Graham's phrase. And a little of it can go a long way toward building your internal network, especially with people you may not work with directly.

Small Talk in Job Interviews

There can be a real value to small talk for all parties in job interview situations. Here are some suggestions.

For the Candidate

It's understandable that the screening and interview process can make candidates nervous. When you're in the hot seat, you're not always given much information about who you're meeting, or why; you're trying to take in a lot of information at once; and you might endure four, five, or six back-to-back (or worse, group) meetings in one day. The achievement you have to unlock during this stressful routine is to win over a majority of those you meet. It's extremely daunting. So as a candidate, do your best to glean extra information from the recruiter, or between meetings, via the magic of small talk (*Thank you so much for having me in. Am I meeting with anyone we haven't talked about yet?*).

Small talk can also boost the signal about your (presumably keen) interest in the company, the role, the team (*I've been a user/ customer for years, I always notice the ads, I'm excited about that acquisition you're making*). Integrating small talk should incorporate your awareness about the company: congratulate interviewers about company recognition; refer knowledgeably to the latest product news, their activities in charitable giving and community affairs, their social media strategy. Of course, you'll go into detail during the interview, but these asides indicate your enthusiasm and how the company aligns with your interests and values.

As for personal small talk, as a candidate you want to be judicious—this isn't the time for oversharing. A brief mention in passing of your passion for sports or animals can be fine if there's some relationship to the overall conversation. But the job interview is more about highlighting your professional capabilities.

For the Interviewer

Tech companies usually have hiring panels consisting of a variety of people who are likely to work with the role being filled. Each one who meets a candidate gives feedback and scores (something the company sets), which add up during the decision to hire. Over the last couple of decades, I've interviewed scores of candidates for all kinds of roles using this kind of process. I might be an introvert, but I'm also empathic and solicitous; part of my job is to represent the company well and to make these visitors feel comfortable. En route to the meeting room, I'll unfailingly be a small-talker: *Were the directions clear? Did you come far? Is this a busy week for you?* I might also toss off a few observations about the office—why it's noisy or quiet, messy or neat; I'll point out anything interesting on the walls, offer a drink, show them the view.

Aside from putting people at ease—which, as we've seen, small talk can accomplish—these quick (and usually forgettable) exchanges give me clues about candidates:

- Do their responses include personal insights that go beyond the standard back-and-forth?
- Are they long-winded, inexplicably cheerful, overly nervous or apologetic, trenchant, self-referential in the extreme?
- Do they appear curious and engaged, or offhanded and distracted?

Such meta-information lets me begin to gauge their ability to be flexible, or clever, or distant, or—you get the idea. And any behavior provides a sense of how they might fit into the particular team they would be working with and the context of the work. When approached this way, all of what you get during your brief meeting can provide a good sense of someone you wouldn't get if you were completely focused on how a candidate "performs" on a checklist of topics. Small talk offers an opportunity to demonstrate curiosity, passion, critical and creative thinking skills, wide-ranging life experiences; these are the qualities I think most of us doing the hiring want to see.

Afterward, and of course without making any commitment about their prospects, I offer a couple of safe closers: *You must be looking forward to the weekend, I hope traffic isn't too bad, I'm glad we could spend a little time together.* I might compliment their style, which is meant to signal to someone with a tattoo, pink suede booties, or blue-tipped hair that we at the company value such individuality.

TRY IT OUT: Be Careful with Small Talk

Interviewers must walk a fine line with prospective candidates. You want to make everyone feel comfortable, but there are social "don'ts" as well as questions that are illegal to ask. A few guidelines:

- Make compliments lightly, with care and sincerity.
- Avoid enthusiastic praise, and never focus on gender specifics (for example, a male interviewer should not compliment a woman candidate's looks or clothing, and vice versa).
- Stay neutral about the state of the search and the candidate's standing.
- Be positive ("I enjoyed our conversation"), but don't promise anything ("We'll be in touch").

I should add that as an older woman, and someone who is inclusive by nature, I'm probably in a safer position than many others to genuinely appreciate and compliment all kinds of people I meet. If you're not, or you don't have the luxury of age, tread lightly. Be sure you understand the impact of your role, age, gender, and standing in the company in relation to the candidate *before* you attempt to give any compliments.

Team Small Talk

Another area for work-related small talk is when a team is out of its usual routine, say at an offsite meeting or during an impromptu social moment like sharing a birthday. These sometimes awkward get-togethers are not the time to be all business or standoffish. A modest amount of socializing and personalizing (your upcoming vacation plans, a funny thing the baby did, passing around a latest pet video, your mom's visit) becomes a useful lubricant in the moment. Sharing small personal tidbits of information gives people a good feeling about others, making it easier in the future to collaborate and communicate across the group. When people like each other and have traded somewhat inconsequential tidbits, work tends to go more easily, with a stronger sense of camaraderie.

As someone who has worked for years around people who are generally two or even three decades younger than me, small talk serves as a bridge over what might otherwise be a big gap. I'm happy to inquire and make small talk about my colleagues' weekend plans and current cultural passions—it helps me understand how they tick and how to work with them. For their part, I think they appreciate my interest in their doings, especially since I absolutely *never* try to match stories or compete for youth points. (I'd lose.) In their eyes I'm a friendly, generically older, and anomalous creature who seems to keep up well enough. For this reason, I skip nostalgic mentions about the "old days" (music, concerts, cost of schooling, etc.) and avoid too much self-disclosure. This strategy works beautifully for introverts as well as older employees, by the way, which is a bonus.

Small Talk in Social Situations

When I'm invited to something that's loosely professional but not required—say, a book party, an evening presentation, a corporate announcement—small talk continues to help me out. I like to establish ahead of time that at least one or two people I know will also be there, which eases any low-level anxiety about making the effort to go. And I do enjoy observing group behavior, which will be on display. The first thing I do when I arrive is size up the room: where the drinks and food are, which seat should I grab (usually on an aisle or near a door for me, thanks). Then I'll make a quick circuit to get a sense of the space and the people there. With people I recognize, I'll manage a little small talk, usually with a couple of "what's new?" questions geared to whatever the context is (are we there for a technology reveal, a media presentation, an industry overview?).

After making that circuit—very different than working the room, since I'm not there for any transactions—I seek out a quiet corner. If I do have one or two friends there, we might have a genuine (but short) tête-à-tête before the presentation. I'll listen and take notes during the main program, and then, having made time for a few interesting moments and one or two direct connections, I head for the exit. Mission accomplished!

Making Small Talk Online

Finally, there is a newer avenue for small talk: in online conversation, which I define broadly as email, chat, on Twitter, or in private messages. I talk about these in chapter 6 in some detail, so here I simply want to mention that online, social small talk can make it a lot easier to reach out to strangers or weak-tie contacts, as well as keep up with friends. Having observed someone's public social postings, for example, can give you an opening to reach out with a short, friendly icebreaker before you get to your point. Whether they're reading, seeing, or hearing these conversational gambits, I think people appreciate the effort you make to express interest and awareness of them and their world. As for people you know and like, online small talk can be no more than a "What's up?" ping, a short expression when you pass along news of mutual interest.

To sum it all up, sometimes small talk is necessary, sometimes it's advisable, and sometimes it's the best way to send friendly signals to a fellow human. I hope this chapter encourages you to try it now and again and dread it a little less. With luck, it might persuade you that you're not required to get a personality transplant to conduct your life, and brief social exchanges can be useful, if not momentarily pleasurable.

Nuts and Bolts of the Job Hunt

> If we wait for the moment when everything,
> absolutely everything, is ready, we shall never begin.
> —*Ivan Turgenev*

One very real-world situation few of us can escape is the process of hunting for a new job. One of the reasons continuous networking has become so vital is that people are perennially on the lookout. In a 2017 study on the American workplace, Gallup reported that 51 percent of Americans holding jobs are also actively searching for new ones, or at least keeping an eye on openings. That means there's virtually always competition, so the smartest strategy is to stay in the game by keeping your contacts "warm" and current. In this chapter we'll explore how to use the power of connections in your quest for the next gig, and how to make the process work better for you.

The Reality of Job Listings

There's no shortage of online job sites—both the broad ones you search by keyword, title, and location, and numerous specialty sites that list jobs by field or industry. It's worth regularly checking a few of your favorite sites to discover and research new listings that appeal to you. In addition to LinkedIn, the standard-bearers among the major wide-ranging job and career sites include Indeed.com, Glassdoor, CareerBuilder, Monster.com, and SimplyHired. Then there are others that aggregate jobs in one sector—for example, Idealist.org, Philanthropy.com, and Bridgespan cover nonprofit positions; SchoolSpring and Edjoin stick to educational openings; Dice offers technical listings; TalentZoo and Krop gather advertising and marketing positions. Still others like SimplyHired encourage diversity by promoting listings for people with disabilities, including veterans. Your favorite search engine will show you lots more.

By all means dig in to all the sites that speak to you and pursue those companies and job descriptions you like. *But don't stop there.* When you see openings that appeal to you, you have two immediate tasks:

1. Do research on the company.
2. Find anyone you know who is connected to the company.

The first is imperative to understand all the aspects of a business: how it makes money—the organizational structure, competitors, products, and services—and equally important, its mission, values, and reputation, what the culture is like. You want to feel good about the businesses you're pursuing across all of these dimensions (or be very clear about what you're willing to sacrifice to get in). The more you treat these target companies as a kind of journalistic enterprise, the better. Get to know the who, what, where, when, why, and how of the business—and go beyond the bounds of the actual job opening you want.

The second task is equally crucial, and it's where networking really matters: you want to find personal connections in, or close to, the companies you're investigating. According to employment

site Jobvite, *referrals are five times more likely to lead to an offer* than simply sending in a resume. It's become common for employers to offer various incentives, including cash bonuses to employees whose referrals lead to new hires. (Such incentives also cut down on what employers need to spend on advertising and search firms—and it's a nice perk for people you know to help you land a job.) Beyond the referral process, the connections you make with people who work in, or have worked in or done business with, your target company can sharpen your understanding of the place. I've fielded scores of requests from

> Get to know the who, what, where, when, why, and how of the company, beyond the specifics of the job you want.

people who want intel on a company I know about, which I am always happy to give. Whether or not I'm a fan of the company, I aim to understand where the asker is in their career—sometimes two or three years in a relevant role at a not-so-great company with a name brand, for example, might be beneficial.

And if I don't happen to know enough about a particular division or team but know someone who does, I'll pass along an introduction so the candidate can be even better informed. That would go something like this: I send a short note summarizing who's interested, including their LinkedIn profile or personal website. I'll also mention their expertise as an extra detail to jump-start my friend's thinking, e.g.: *Joe's background in business development at [relevant company] seems like a good fit for [your company]*, or *Ellen's ten years of doing partnerships in Asia could be useful as your company expands to that region.* To close the note, I'll ask: *May I introduce you, or can you point me or him to someone else in the know?*

It's an old line, but it continues to be true: information is power. This is a way to gather yours.

Beyond Job Listings

Then there are the companies you're interested in, but they show no current listings that reflect your skills. Why would that be? There are a host of reasons: an opening exists, but there's a hiring freeze; the employer is small and can't afford paid listings (reminder: check the company's own site); poor performers must be eased out before new postings appear; internal discussions about reorganization and revamped or new roles can take months, which means a hold on new openings—you get the idea.

If you're not in a hurry, not seeing an interesting opening at a place you'd like to work isn't necessarily a dead end—and it's where connections can play a big role. As an example, I have a journalist friend I'll call Eleanor with a successful career writing for magazines and newspapers. Now in her forties, she's interested in applying skills she's gained in audio and video storytelling at a digital platform like Twitter, Instagram, or Snapchat, among others. She understands that there are only a handful of such roles at these tech-driven services, so for now she simply wants to establish contacts at each place. That's a smart approach. Open-ended conversations will help shape her thinking about exactly what she'd like to do and how to position herself. She's set up news alerts for the companies that interest her and continues to solicit introductions to learn about other places that might be a good fit. As future positions open in the companies she's looking into, she'll be in line to apply through the people she already knows.

Sometimes companies start out a new search by hiring people for a project, or in a time-limited contract role. This can be a great way for all parties to get acquainted, as well as demonstrate that the work might become full-time. I've been a contractor many times and have frequently hired them, too. The way things start goes something like this: *We're facing new product launch/initiative/deadline and we need extra hands. Who on the team knows a writer/photographer/project manager/video producer/IT pro (etc.) who can come in?* It really pays to already have inside contacts; usually these temp and contractor roles aren't posted—it's all about friends of friends.

This is exactly how I began working at Google. I had stayed in touch with a friend who had joined the funny-sounding startup in 1999. When the original dot-com crash hit the Bay Area in 2000–2001, I had already been through two companies closing, and was on the hunt for freelance work. I got in touch with my friend, who told me that Google, which in 2002 employed about five hundred people, was short-handed; they needed marketing writers. I began freelancing exclusively there in 2002, and after fifteen months of trying to make myself indispensable, there was finally approval to add "head count"—a new full-time salaried position for the work I was already doing. Playing a waiting game is how I got hired there.

This scenario might not suit a job seeker who needs to maintain health coverage or other benefits, but it's a way in for those who have the ability to try on a job for size. Take, for example, an energetic friend I'll call Georgia, a seasoned event producer. About two years ago, she had a full-time job that was fine for the time being, but she knew she wanted to make a move. Her top choice was to join a very well-known global company. Through her connections, she had a couple of get-acquainted meetings with several people there. They liked her but had no suitable roles at her level or the necessary head count. Georgia held on to her full-time job and stayed in close touch with her contacts. After a few months, her dream employer told her that they wanted her to come in as a contractor for a major global event—a few months' work—and, assuming everything worked out, they could convert her to full-time within a year. Based on the relationships she'd developed with the team, Georgia trusted them enough to take the leap. Fortunately for her (and the company), it all worked out. Now she has very happily converted to full-time at a place where she wants to be.

Taking an Independent Turn

As we've discussed earlier, there's a growing world of freelance and consulting work for those who want to remain independent— people who want to hang out a shingle to consult and go from project to project for a variety of clients. This is the path I took after leaving Twitter in 2016. It seemed like a good time to put myself out there as an editorial consultant, given my years of experience. When you go independent, the network you've been nurturing all along plays a vital role. The post I wrote announcing my new stint led to nearly two months of meetings, coffee dates, and meals with many people—some strangers, some I knew slightly, and quite a few friends or friendly acquaintances—in a position to hire me. The result of meeting so many people then led to a nice, rich stew of project work that has sustained me since.

In addition to work-related meetings, I've made sure to say yes to agenda-less introductions, which has led to more referrals. Having no agenda was key to the creation of this book, in fact, I didn't have a specific idea when things began to unfold; each conversation led to the next step.

- **August 2015**: Steven Levy $\rightarrow$ published my post on networking
- **January 2017**: Tim Leberecht $\rightarrow$ introduced me to his book editor

- **February 2017**: Hollis Heimbouch → suggested I talk to an agent
- **February 2017**: Raju Narisetti → introduced me to his agent friend
- **November 2017**: Lynn Johnston → sold my book to Touchstone

I've added the dates to show you that time is an important element of networking. Not everything can unfold at once, or in a tidy way. This is how new opportunities come to life.

When independent editor Caroline Pincus (note: I found her through my network to help me develop this book) returned to consulting after a long in-house stint with a publisher, she immediately contacted her many publishing colleagues, as well as several of the editorial assistants she had hired over the years, each of whom, she notes, "now have successful publishing careers, and now regularly refer clients to me." Of course, she also reached out to many of the authors she had worked with, and they, too, became important sources of referral.

As our stories illustrate, keeping in loose touch with your contacts is what it's all about—when there's no immediate job, when you want to build a relationship with people inside a company, when the formulation of roles and needs isn't yet shaken out. I should add that even though Caroline and I both have years under our belts, you can certainly go out on your own at an earlier age, especially if you're willing to put time into making ongoing connections. Having personal relationships and checking in with a spirit of openness and flexibility can lead you to new opportunities that literally no one had thought about before you came along.

Moving to the Next Level

There's another kind of quest that takes longer than nailing a new job right away: building your profile for future returns by making new connections and becoming better known in your field. This is where Abby Kearns finds herself. With more than fifteen years of enterprise software and operations expertise—managing technical teams and delivering complex projects, developing and executing product and business strategies—Abby has serious chops in an industry that has long overlooked women and even been unwelcoming to them. I recently met her at the request of a mutual friend, who wants to help her become more visible in her area.

Today there's greater industry-wide interest in professionals like Abby than there used to be. Why? Because now hiring executives, conference planners, and corporate boards are all keenly aware of the benefits of diversity and inclusion. Recent research from global consulting firm McKinsey shows that companies with meaningful diversity in gender and race (if not age!) among employees at all levels see better financial performance than those that don't. Besides that, a growing number of organizations have been uncomfortably aware of the reputational hit they take if they don't step up in this arena.

So, after years of playing behind the scenes, Abby—who strikes me as eminently capable and admits to being somewhat of an introvert—feels ready to become better known. Being more visible will help headhunters and conference organizers find her, which will lead to opportunities that help her move up in her field. As she recently said to me, "I figured, Why not follow up to make coffee dates? Even if I don't know *why* I should meet, more often than not I get an interesting conversation out if it." Since Abby's goals at the moment are open-ended, they require ongoing one-to-one connections with any number of people.

The same might be true for you: the more people you know personally who are aware of your skills, the more you'll be top of mind for all kinds of opportunities. I realize there's a lot of conditional language here, but that's because this is a longer game than the basic job hunt. Each encounter may bring some reward. Here are a few tactics to help you play your own long game:

- **Broaden** your LinkedIn Summary. This is what appears at the top of your page. It can (and arguably should) be a broader reflection of your abilities and interests, and where you're aiming, than the chronological entries below.

- **Write and post** about professional topics. To illuminate your thinking about the work you do, what your passions are, your observations about your field, and similar topics, write posts and share them. LinkedIn and Medium are two good places to do this, because other people in your orbit will read and pass them along.

- **Let others know of your interest** in being an advisor to a startup, pursuing a leadership role on boards, or other roles that raise your visibility. These roles are rarely advertised, so people in your orbit(s) are the best conduit.

- **Volunteer with charitable organizations** you care about that relate to your professional life. For example, if you work in the software industry, becoming active with organizations that help young women gain technical skills, such as Girls Who Code, Black Girls Code, or other STEM programs, adds to your professional profile. Or if you work in a business that supports on-the-job training or internships, become active with those corporate affairs efforts.

Don't Just Attend Conferences, Speak at Them

Looking for spots where you can speak or present at conferences is a great way to get noticed and start building your own platform.

- Seek out conferences where your expertise makes you a desirable speaker. *Pro tip, especially for women, people of color, and LGBTQ folks*: many conference organizers know they need to diversify their speaker lineup (and their audiences).
- Small conferences and seminars tend to be more informal and less daunting than big trade shows. You stand a better chance here of making more than passing connections.
- At smaller events, offer to convene or moderate breakout sessions that demonstrate your abilities to lead and collaborate.
- A stretch goal, where applicable: push to be a keynoter. (Lots of keynote presentations today run a manageable twenty or thirty minutes—very different from the hour-long stemwinders of the past.) Keynotes give you extra clout and material to build your trajectory.

There Might Be an App for That

Even though I preach throughout this book about personal connections, I'd be remiss not to mention the fact that you can also find a number of apps designed to help you with various aspects of business networking. I've not tried most of them (and confess I'm not likely to), but I don't want to dismiss them out of hand—you might find one or more useful. There are a couple of broad categories to look into: *contacts enhancement* tools make the most sense for introverts. You can keep your contacts current, and their information appears in a handy app or as an email-adjacent add-on, all without having to bother anybody for updates. See, for example, FullContact, CircleBack, Sync.ME, or Cloze. Another approach some apps have taken is to *connect people around professional interests* (no, not for dating!). These sorts of apps are designed to connect you with people who share your professional background or interests, sometimes within conferences, so you can make new connections. See for example Shapr, Bizzabo, Bumble Bizz, or CityHour.

In reading this chapter, you might have found yourself wondering if this book is about networking or job hunting. The answer is that the former serves the latter, which is why I've veered slightly into some of the mechanics of a job search. Taking the next step in your professional life can be stressful, so if you've been nurturing your connections, you're far more likely to find your way.

Remember, everyone you know, have met in passing, or even follow online is a potential connector to others and a potential link to job leads. Everything we've discussed so far comes into play: weak ties, keeping in loose touch, your online toolkit, and so forth. Use all of it to follow the leads that speak to you, and the right opportunity is bound to come.

— 12 —

You've Got This

Liberation does not come from outside.
—*Gloria Steinem*

As you think about how to reclaim networking for yourself, I understand there are plenty of reasons to resist connecting with people you don't know well. Especially when you feel doubtful about your career trajectory, or lost as you attempt to try something new, it's daunting. When you're feeling vulnerable, you don't think you warrant the time and attention of people in the know. Most everyone feels this way at a crossroads, whether it's the next step on the job ladder, a physical move, or a pivot in career or education.

This chapter addresses some of those fears. I hope it can serve as a bit of a pep talk from someone who has known her share of self-doubt. Especially when I was younger, I was very tentative about my skills and aspirations. I tended to set low-ceiling limits for what I could do or how far I could go. (Don't mind me, I'm fine over here in the corner.) It took years of just plain living—and yes, therapy—to feel solidly planted, to understand that I'm fine as is, that I can meet anyone as an equal. I'm here to gently remind you that if I can do it, you can, too. You can build yourself a bigger safety net with more meaningful connections to people you can call on when you need to, and even help others along your path.

The Struggle Is Real

To be sure, you may encounter, as we all do, dispiriting obstacles along your way. If you're fifty or older, you are probably not imagining age discrimination—it can be very real. (Friends in their forties tell me even they feel the chilly wind of ageism, but for our purposes, the fifties are a tipping point.) As for women, we sometimes limit ourselves too much around job searches and even around our goals. Then there are people of any age and gender who understandably feel a setback when they move to a new city, set out to learn new skills, or yearn to change fields. Any of these goals and needs can unleash a sense of vulnerability, and that in turn leads us (yes, I've done this) to minimize our own needs. These days, when I meet with people in all of these situations who have come to see me because they would like fresh ideas or contacts, I sometimes hear this kind of backpedaling on the spot:

- "I don't want to be a bother."
- "I'm not really ready to meet anyone right now; I need to do my homework first."
- "I'd better wait till I have my resume/portfolio together."

There can, of course, be legitimate reasons to hold off on introductions or follow-through, but more often than not, I think these are stalling tactics. My main argument against delay is this: *The people you should meet next are not the ones doing the hiring.* You don't need to have your resume (or your act) together for them. The contacts I'm suggesting might be in a related field, have gone through a similar search, or know a lot about your desired company or industry. For you potential procrastinators, here are two reminders:

1. *It's just coffee.* Having a low-stress cafe meeting is a mutual hour of getting-to-know-you. It's going to be informative in some way, maybe even if it convinces you to avoid that role or company.
2. I'm sure you'd agree to help another person asking you for time to brainstorm career ideas. *Aren't you worthy of the same help?* As Gloria Steinem has said, "Look for allies everywhere. Do not be bound by conventional hierarchies."

Now let's take a closer look at some of these obstacles you might be facing.

A Word to All the Sisters

Speaking of Steinem, I can't recall a time when a guy asking me for ideas has then backpedaled to say he "doesn't want to be a bother." Women, though—whether they are friends of mine, strangers, acquaintances, from all kinds of backgrounds—will often say they aren't ready for contacts and guidance, even *in the moment when they really need them.* Hello, sisters! I know you're familiar with what has been called "the confidence gap"—that phenomenon in which women may over-prepare, worrying that they're not "good enough," not ready for that next step, while men are comfortable winging an interview or embellishing their experience, all while exuding the confidence that leads to a positive outcome. In a 2014 report, *The Atlantic* cited a study from HP (formerly Hewlett-Packard) which found that their women employees applied for a promotion "only when they believed they met 100 percent of the qualifications listed for the job. Men were happy to apply when they thought they could meet 60 percent of the job requirements."

Sound familiar? It's no surprise to see the same phenomenon around networking and making new connections. Take Eileen (not her real name), a woman I've known for years. She has a successful track record conducting research and market testing for major consumer clients. Given the cyclical nature of her projects, we get together during her work lulls to brainstorm about new leads for her to pursue. She always agrees with me about who she *could*, or *should*, meet with—but also has confided that reaching out makes her "feel a bit of shame, like I'm begging because I'm professionally impoverished." While she recognizes this might be "silly," using her word, she struggles: "Emotionally, I should have it more together." Her hesitation captures the feeling many women seem to have when they want new ideas, and especially when they don't know where to turn.

In tracing this confidence gap further back, it's easy to see how underconfident women might delay in acting on their interest in a new role or a new field, overthinking or getting into the weeds too early. Plenty of women I know have a deep-seated belief—and I have struggled with this one, too—that we're *never* "ready enough" for even an informal introduction or initial contact. Memo to all the Eileens (and Karens): an informal meeting with a potential connection is not a job interview. It's a conversation with someone who might be helpful. (Then again, it might be a pleasant dead end, and off you go to the next get-together.) Don't make the stakes so high that you freeze up. Even if you spend forty-five minutes deducing that the person, the role, the company (take your pick) seem awful, that's a win—it will save you a lot of time later! The important point here, in case it needs repeating, is first, that *you are worth the effort*, and second, *just keep moving*. There's no time like the present to start making new inroads.

> An informal meeting with a potential connection is not a job interview. It's just a conversation with someone who might be helpful.

If You're Just Getting Started

Though I've written a good deal about people who are already working, and who have some kind of network because they have work history, when should you start? When I meet new college graduates, interns, or others searching for their first professional job, I encourage them to get used to the idea of reaching out to people, informally, as they make their way into the world of work. *There's no better time than now to start connecting.* Your own school friends are your contacts, as are their parents you're friendly with, your teachers, any mentors you've already met, your summer employers, places where you've volunteered and interned.

In addition to staying in touch with contacts you know, get in the habit of asking people who seem interesting and talented for an informational coffee date just to hear their story and tell them yours. Then make a point to keep up with them now and again to touch base about your experiences and to hear about theirs. Before long, you will have a nice group of connections for yourself and can even help others right behind you. Human resources journalist Tony Lee reminds new grads that "an effective networking relationship helps both parties. Contacts enjoy talking about themselves, how they got jobs after college and how companies in their industry are doing. And if they can match you up with a job somewhere, they're doing both you and your new employer a favor that they hope will be returned one day. It's a win-win situation."

If You're "Old" Like Me

Let me take a few moments to speak with the fifty-pluses among you, since you're probably feeling the need to hone your skills to stay in the game. A 2018 study from job search service Career-

Builder reported that 53 percent of workers who are sixty years old are postponing retirement, and 4 in 10 don't know when they'll retire. If "sixty is the new forty"—a nod to the millions of Baby Boomers now in, or fast approaching, our sixties and seventies—when it comes to work opportunities, the older you get, the less you matter in the workforce. For one thing, past fifty you've become an expensive resource (you make a higher salary, have earned more paid leave, may have more expensive health care costs, and so on). In large companies, efficiency experts regularly calculate the buyout package to get you out the door. If you're part of the old guard with years of seniority, it's true you have great institutional knowledge—but the value of that shrinks over time, as companies undertake new strategies and require new skills. Wherever you sit, your days may be numbered, or at least you've hit a ceiling.

Beyond the higher cost of fifty-plus workers, there are other factors at play. I've met many people with solid twenty- or thirty-year careers whose fields are undergoing major upheavals (publishing, retail, and so on), trying to figure out how to get into something new. Another reason is family changes (caretaking, kids, older relatives) that may require a physical move; that can lead to a lot of unknowns about next steps. And of course some fifty-plus people would like an on-ramp to more flexible work hours so they can eventually scale back.

It's easy to understand the reluctance these and other "older" people have about meeting strangers, especially those who might be younger and may represent the change they fear. Not unreasonably, the older worker might think: *Why would they help me? What will we have to talk about? What if they say no?* I've seen quite a few work veterans set their sights lower—or stay in a stale longtime role, playing the waiting game for a severance package—because of such fears.

Age discrimination is a kind of gaslight phenomenon. There's a lot you don't see or know, and most of the time very little that you can prove. Certainly in the tech world, which has seized the collective imagination as being exclusively for those under thirty, no one is going to directly say, "You're too old to fit in here." Though it's not been my own Silicon Valley experience, age discrimination does exist. But because it's usually not overt (especially when you initially apply for a job), practically speaking, there's not a lot you can do about it.

What you *can* do, though, is homework—that is, research. For example:

- Look closely at the diversity and inclusion record of companies you're interested in (it will be rare to find a word on age, but look anyway).
- Search LinkedIn to see if people in your age range work there, and make connections to get a reality check.
- Search news stories and commentary to discover any efforts either to include or exclude fifty-plus workers (a recent negative example is IBM, which has come under fire for forcing out longtime employees).
- Candidly assess your own tolerance for change, especially if it means working in a place where you're not likely to get pride of place due to age or experience. (Some people can embrace chaos and the unknown more easily than others.)

If you get an opportunity to interview at a new place, be your most wise, alert, and interesting self at every step. Your experience and earned wisdom are very real assets, and they do have value—even if you can't play them up as your primary credentials. Typically, young companies zero in on what you can do for them instead of what you've done before. That's not a bad formulation for you to follow. In doing your homework about the field and the company, think about how your experience and skills address specific needs they have. Do they need to expand internationally, develop partnership programs, build more training programs? Your experience may fit those needs. Over my years in tech, I've often been praised for my calm perspective, ability to "get shit done" as the saying goes (it's a compliment), and be a trusted sounding board. That's all nice to hear, but I find myself thinking, *I'm good at those things because I'm old! I've been around the block! Few things faze me anymore!*

I didn't join Google until I was fifty-one; I was sixty when I joined Twitter. I learned an immense amount at both places, but I will tell you that it took fortitude to stay positive and fully motivated every day. That's not because I experienced overt discrimination; it's more about my expectations (initially, I believed my past experience would automatically elevate me) versus the reality of working in a dynamic young environment, where learning on the job and making mistakes are part of the landscape. Ultimately, I benefited greatly from this system, though I believe that young workers get a lot more latitude than older ones to learn the ropes and "fail fast." Since the recruiting emphasis in companies needing a lot of fresh technical talent is on college grads and twenty-somethings, I don't expect a dramatic shift in attitudes.

I had worked around tech companies for years prior, but they were all relatively small organizations. Even in Google's early period, hiring ramped up considerably: I arrived in the fall of 2002, when there were under six hundred employees; less than two years later, there were twenty-three hundred. By the time I left in 2011, there were fifty thousand. Those of us in the trenches had to learn very quickly to deal with this rapid influx of newbies, which also brought increased structure, more management layers, and lots of process.

During this high-growth phase it pained me deeply that I didn't advance as quickly as I expected, especially in contrast to people I viewed as peers—not because they were younger (which they were), but because their roles were more valued by the company. I'd concocted my editorial role largely by myself; I didn't have a champion who wanted to help me ascend. I understood that it would never be as highly valued as a role deemed more central to the company, especially product or engineering.

Nevertheless, I put my feelings aside to get what I could out of a name-brand employer. That turned out to be wonderfully life-changing. I thrived at our breathless pace with lively, smart, younger comrades. But especially in their go-go years, such corporations may not be the right step if you're used to all the perks in a more traditional industry. I've talked quite a few people out of "getting into tech" if they seem too attached to their career-long recognition and expect it will carry over to this new world—it's no guarantee of success. More broadly, sometimes a company's style just won't suit you. It's less about young-versus-old than it is about what the company's values are, or the business it's in.

An efficient way to learn about a new industry or pick up a variety of skills quickly is to join a specialist consulting agency (for example, marketing and advertising, tech support, communications) that has clients across a range of businesses. Or you might consider roles in firms that are not brand names, less well-known companies outside the spotlight where you can get the skills you need to transition into a new area.

Two more points about the need to network when you're in the fifty-plus club. One, the longer you've worked (and lived), the more contacts you'll have from a wide variety of backgrounds. Remember your weak ties? These are especially useful as you explore new options and locations. Think very broadly about who you know, including people you may have met in passing or who are colleagues of friends, to learn about opportunities that are not familiar.

Second, think about how you can position yourself as a "mentern"—a neologism that describes someone who can *mentor* others while learning new skills as an intern does (not that you have to actually be in that role). In his book *Wisdom @ Work: The Making of a Modern Elder*, the seasoned hotelier and entrepreneur Chip Conley tells the story of joining Airbnb at age fifty-two. Though Chip has earned plenty of EQ (emotional intelligence) over his career, he says he came to the young company with no discernible DQ (digital intelligence). As he tells it, his time at Airbnb helped him gain DQ as he was able to impart EQ to younger colleagues. A similar fictional tale is told in the 2015 film *The Intern*, in which Robert De Niro plays an unflappable seventy-year-old widower who becomes an assistant to the rather anxious and much younger CEO, played by Anne Hathaway, at a fast-growing tech company. Naturally, he learns new office skills as he teaches her and her team a good deal about being productive and effective with less stress and better people skills. As Chip did, and as the movie illustrates, you're in a good position to do similar work in a new environment.

If Your Network Is Dormant

When people are in the same organization or on the same team for many years, they get comfortable. Maybe they don't plan to leave their familiar (even familial) environment. But—things happen. You might be bored. You might not have a good feeling about the new head of your team or company. You notice you're envious of friends moving into new positions. Then there are those who have been out of the job market for any number of reasons: caretaking for children or parents, a serious illness, a difficult divorce, legal troubles. I recently met a woman in her forties with solid technical skills who had been off the market for two years, caring for each of her parents and in-laws as they declined and died. (She was once again making the rounds to find work and had to explain her recent absence. I fervently hope she's gotten offers as well as sympathy.) After the shock of change comes the time to renew yourself and rev that professional engine again.

Not long ago I met a woman I'll call Alice—an experienced communications executive. She'd held her current role for ten years and has recognized that she's gotten bored. And being in one place for so long, she confided to me, she'd let her network go. Now she needed new contacts in order to look around for a new position. Ideally, she wouldn't have let her contacts go dormant in the first place. As you know by now, at any stage of work life, you should regularly nurture your contacts. Today Alice is making up for her missing network by creating a new one: she's connecting regularly with new people and getting new leads. She follows up with each one, and also with those of us who have made introductions so that we also stay informed about her progress. I have every confidence that Alice will find a great new position that suits her while she's at her current job. And I bet she never lets her contacts go dormant again.

When Life Comes at You

A prime time when networking becomes paramount is during any kind of life transition. You may be just starting your work life without much of a road map. (That was me, a diehard liberal-arts type.) Or you may have some career years in hand but are facing planned or unplanned changes. Wherever you are in the labyrinth, facing some kind of unknown brings on the fog of unfamiliarity and fosters anxiety. Whether it's a graduation or a layoff, a divorce or separation, a necessary move, a birth or death—they all require you to reach outside your circle to learn from new acquaintances. Life changes call for us to develop new routines and cultivate new ideas. If you don't, you risk closing in and limiting your future options for work and growth.

A favorite "life comes at you" story is about my friend Sree Sreenivasan. A couple of years ago, he was unexpectedly forced out of a wonderful job he'd held for three years as the first chief digital officer for the Metropolitan Museum of Art in New York City, having fallen victim to the museum's financial troubles. More than most of us, Sree, who's been a journalist, social media innovator, and professor at Columbia University, has cultivated a large and lively following, both online and in the real world. When news of his departure appeared, I assumed he'd turn privately to some well-placed contacts and lock in his next gig behind the scenes. But Sree took his job search public, letting his many followers know that he was open to hearing about leads from all comers. He even posted an open Google Doc to capture ideas and contacts anyone wanted to offer; he invited people to join him on walking "get acquainted" meetups (sometimes called walk-and-talks) around New York City. He took a new role with the City of New York, which turned out to be a short stint: the position he'd been hired for ended up being merged with another one. Since then, Sree has reinvented himself as a digital and social media consultant, building on his well-established and active presence on Facebook, where he hosts several groups, LinkedIn, Twitter, and Instagram, as well as his extensive personal network. Today he has a full schedule of workshops, speaking and consulting with organizations across the world. It's quite possibly a perfect role for him after his wild ride during the last few years. As he has observed about that ride, "You need an incredible support group, and people who understand. *You have to build it when you don't need it*" (my emphasis).

Even for those without the large network Sree enjoys, his recent journey offers some good lessons for the rest of us:

- Change comes whether or not you're expecting it.
- (Therefore!) keep yourself open to new possibilities.
- You always know more people than you think you know.
- Tell your story and be clear about what you need.

My best advice to you in changing times is to chip away steadily at your uncertainties by reaching out to old and new acquaintances—especially your weak ties—for a call, chat, walk, or coffee date to learn a little from each one. No one person, no one meeting, is likely to give you a single perfect answer, but all that you learn will become parts of *your* answer. It's how you'll frame your thinking about new opportunities.

Finally, as you contemplate change and conquering old habits, try this thought on: to build a lasting network, you should aim to be generous not only with others, but also with yourself. Most of us would gladly help someone else who needs counsel, but all too often we're reluctant to get that support for ourselves. Revered UCLA basketball coach John Wooden famously lived by a seven-point creed. The point that applies best to the downhearted job seeker, the career aspirer, and the would-be changemaker is this one: "Build a shelter against a rainy day."

Afterword

Throughout this book I've tried to make the case that networking doesn't have to be a chore, and with luck, it will serve a greater purpose for you than just counting up your contacts. With an open mind and a sense of curiosity about others, you'll see the benefits of connection throughout your life.

The reason I'm such a believer about this idea is that I've experienced it ever since I landed in the San Francisco Bay Area nearly thirty-five years ago. Even as I was settling in, I felt a sense of permission: this was a place where it was okay to try anything, change my mind, shed old skin. Of course, San Francisco has beckoned to thousands of people in this way for more than a century—it's as if the marine air itself invites openness to new ideas and to reinvention. Writers from Kevin Starr and Rebecca Solnit to Leslie Berlin and John Markoff, among many others, have told the captivating stories that reveal the long arc of this regional sense of openness. As one pilgrim among generations who have come, I saw that the Bay Area would be a good and safe place to be able to change course, disappear, reappear, evolve—and feel accepted at every turn. I learned that change can be a virtue, and equally important, failure isn't a sin. As Stanford business professor Chip Heath put it, "Failure doesn't black-mark your record, especially in Silicon Valley. To fail here is almost a badge of honor. It means you've learned something."

I'm recalling this part of my story because I think this "why not?" spirit is much more pervasive everywhere today than it used to be. The Bay Area, or more narrowly, Silicon Valley, doesn't have a lock on people who aim to pursue self-discovery and reinvention. Among many examples, we're seeing people connect in powerful ways, from the near-spontaneous global Women's Marches in 2017 to the rise of the Village to Village Network for seniors. These and many other human networks have come about because people are connecting to tackle serious and long-standing problems. Equally important, on a personal level, people have more tools than ever before to reach out and keep in touch with one another. Today you can make new connections wherever you are, and convene your brain trust for inspiration and guidance whenever you need it.

The trick when you set out to make new connections is to look beyond that introduction, initial phone call, or meeting. Herbie Hancock has said, "The spirit of jazz is the spirit of openness." So, too, is the art of making genuine connections and learning to improvise with people. As you think about what you need, and who can help, I hope you let that spirit of openness guide you. The answers you need are with you through the people you know a lot or a little, people you'd like to know, and everyone you're open to meeting, maybe for no apparent reason.

Now regroup however you need to, and then open the door.

Acknowledgments

Nothing replaces knowing that your people support you in your endeavors, and in this, I'm a lucky woman. First, thanks must go to technology journalist Steven Levy, who in 2015 offered me room to write on *Backchannel*, his former Medium publication that's now part of Wired.com. Steven encouraged me to publish an essay, "I've Spent a Lifetime Building a Mighty Network," that became the basis for this book. That piece along with other writings led my friend Tim Leberecht to connect me with Hollis Heimbouch, his editor at HarperCollins. My exchanges with Hollis led me to reach out to my superconnector friend Raju Narisetti, which brought me directly to Lynn Johnston, who became my agent. Over a few months' time, Lynn patiently guided me through the arcana of book proposals to win a contract with Touchstone Books. That's how I ended up at the desk of Touchstone Senior Editor Cara Bedick, who has been thoughtful and accessible at every turn. Meanwhile, at home in San Francisco, longtime friend and former colleague Julie Felner introduced me to Caroline Pincus, a seasoned book editor whom I hired to get my ideas (and chapters) into shape for Cara. She proved to be an invaluable first reader and sounding board through months of word wrangling. Everyone needs an editor, I always remind people—even editors like me. I am grateful that I've had two as guides on this long-form adventure.

The Touchstone team, including Shida Carr and Megan Rudloff (publicity), and Kelsey Manning (marketing), and Lara Blackman (editorial), have been invaluable troupers on my behalf. And acknowledgments are never complete without thanking those who put the manuscript into book form; my thanks to copyeditor Patty Romanowski Bashe and production editor Sarah Wright for their diligence.

Other friends and colleagues have been simpatico, and often essential, sounding boards. These include the Lobbinati crew, a small group of sole proprietors who meet monthly to talk shop about consulting and our aspirations: Jennifer Donovan, Julie Felner, David Glickman, Heather O'Donnell, and Dan Tynan. I also got sage advice on framing my ideas from Sara Blask, Vanessa Hope Schneider, Mamie Healey, and Janice Maloney. Betsy Streeter and Nilofer Merchant were early guides in helping me think about the nature of the book; kibitzing over the past year with Walt Mossberg about books, technology, and news literacy also sustained me. Other journalist friends—Geraldine Baum, Dave Beard, Joe Brown, Debbie Weil, Cyndi Stivers, and John House in particular—reminded me that David Carr's maxim ("keep typing until it turns into writing") is timeless for a reason.

As if all this weren't enough, I'm grateful for the unflagging support other good friends have provided. (If you think you're one of these, you are.) A special shout-out goes to those who pinged me regularly to cheer me on, including Eitan Bencuya, Sean Carlson, Christine Chen, Cathy Cook, Shernaz Daver, Tracy DeMiroz, Chris Gaither, Rebecca Goldsmith, Jill Hazelbaker, Amy Hyams, Courtney Hohne, Julie Kim, Brian O'Shaughnessy, Jodi Olson, Barry Owen, Jim Prosser, Maggie Shiels, Gabriel Stricker, Jeff Tidwell, and Aaron Zamost. I'm also grateful to those who agreed to be interviewed: Travis Culwell, Susan Etlinger, Rosie Fantozzi, Tim Fisher, Brian Fitzpatrick, Ann Handley, Abby Kearns,

Alexandra Lange, Ryan McDougall, Ian Sanders, Julie Schlosser, Judy Wert, and Hunter Walk.

Finally, I am dedicating this book to Tom Rielly, my friend of nearly thirty years, with whom I've shared countless adventures, conversations, and travels. From the beginning, Tom showed me how to step past old fears and conventions into a larger life and a world of possibility that grows richer by the day. Love and gratitude, Tom.

Resources

Some of these sources dovetail with my own thinking; others have upended old notions. All of them have informed my approach to this book.

Books

Cain, Susan. *Quiet: The Power of Introverts in a World That Can't Stop Talking*. New York: Broadway Books, 2013.

Clark, Dorie. *Stand Out Networking: A Simple and Authentic Way to Meet People on Your Own Terms*. New York: Penguin, 2015.

Conley, Chip. *Wisdom @ Work: The Making of a Modern Elder*. New York: Currency Books, 2018.

Gerber, Scott, and Ryan Paugh. *Superconnector: Stop Networking and Start Building Business Relationships That Matter*. New York: Da Capo Press, 2018.

Granger, Sarah. *The Digital Mystique: How the Culture of Connectivity Can Empower Your Life—Online and Off*. Berkeley: Seal Press, 2014.

Grant, Adam R. *Give and Take: Why Helping Others Drives Our Success*. New York: Penguin Books, 2013.

Jarvis, Jeff. *Public Parts: How Sharing in the Digital Age Improves the Way We Work and Live*. New York: Simon & Schuster, 2015.

Little, Brian R. *Who Are You, Really? The Surprising Puzzle of Personality*. New York: Simon & Schuster/TED Books, 2017.

Merchant, Nilofer. *The Power of Onlyness: Make Your Wild Ideas Mighty Enough to Dent the World*. New York: Viking, 2017.

Palmer, Amanda. *The Art of Asking: or How I Learned to Stop Worrying and Let People Help*. New York: Grand Central Publishing, 2014.

Stark, Kio. *When Strangers Meet: How People You Don't Know Can Transform You*. New York: Simon & Schuster/TED Books, 2016.

Articles

Benson, David. "The Power of Asynchronous Communication." *The Social Chic* (blog), April 29, 2012.

Blaskie, Erin. "Five Things I Learned About Twitter Bios by Reading Over 4,000 User Profiles." *Medium*, July 24, 2017.

Chambers, Kipp. "Network Is Not a Verb." FullContact.com, July 22, 2015.

Dishman, Lydia. "The Business Etiquette Guide to Emojis." *Fast Company*, July 14, 2016.

Graham, Ruth. "In Defense of Small Talk." *Slate*, February 25, 2016.

Fralic, Chris. "How to Become Insanely Well-Connected." *First Round Review*, April 25, 2017.

Handley, Ann. "How Do You Balance Your Personal and Professional Social Media Presence?" AnnHandley.com, March 2014 (updated March 2018).

Haskell, David George. "Life Is the Network, Not the Self." *Cosmos and Culture* (NPR blog), April 4, 2017.

Ibarra, Herminia, and Mark Lee Hunter. "How Leaders Create and Use Networks." *Harvard Business Review*, January 2007.

Madrigal, Alexis C. "Email Is Still the Best Thing on the Internet." *The Atlantic*, August 14, 2014.

Sreenivasan, Sree. "How to Use Social Media in Your Career." *New York Times*, November 8, 2017.

Steib, Mike. "Don't Just Network—Build Your 'Meaningful Network' to Maximize Your Impact." *First Round Review*, January 23, 2018.

Walk, Hunter. "How This Anxious Introvert Handles Large Events." *Medium*, October 2, 2017.

Sites

Indeed Career Guide: A helpful site covering many topics for job hunting and career planning.

Introvert's Corner Blog, PsychologyToday.com: Lots of material that supports "living a quiet life in a noisy world."

QuietRev.com: The site for Susan Cain's company, with many resources for introverts.

Notes

ix *Collecting the dots.*: Amanda Palmer, *The Art of Asking: or How I Learned to Stop Worrying and Let People Help* (New York: Grand Central Publishing, 2014).

Introduction

1 *Networking is more about farming than it is about hunting.*: Ivan Misner, "The True Definition of Networking," ivanmisner .com (video posted August 18, 2016), http://ivanmisner.com /the-true-definition-of-networking.

2 *a dozen different jobs . . . millennials are projected to hold even more*: "Number of Jobs, Labor Market Experience, and Earnings Growth Among Americans at 50: Results from a Longitudinal Survey," Bureau of Labor Statistics News Release, August 24, 2017, https://www.bls.gov/news.release/pdf/nlsoy.pdf.

2 *twice as many companies . . . than in earlier eras*: Guy Berger, "Will This Year's College Grads Job-Hop More Than Previous Grads?" *LinkedIn* (blog), April 12, 2016, https://blog.linkedin .com/2016/04/12/will-this-year_s-college-grads-job-hop-more -than-previous-grads.

2 *People in the United States move more than eleven times in their lives*: Mona Chalabi, "How Many Times Does the Average Person Move?" *FiveThirtyEight*, January 29, 2015, https://fivethirtyeight .com/features/how-many-times-the-average-person-moves/.

2 *nearly 41 million self-employed Americans aged twenty-one and up*: "The

State of Independence in America 2017: Rising Confidence Amid a Maturing Market," MBO Partners 2017 Report, https://www .mbopartners.com/uploads/files/state-of-independence-reports /StateofIndependence-2017-Final.pdf.

3 *definition of "networking"*: Cambridge Dictionary, https://dictio nary.cambridge.org/us/dictionary/english/networking.

6 *that I was suitably Googley*: A good definition is by (former Googler) Jens Meiert, "The Meanings of Googliness," Meiert .com, August 12, 2013, https://meiert.com/en/blog/googliness/.

PART ONE The Elements of Connecting

9 *When, out of the fear of the unknown, we shut ourselves off from links to one another, we lose as individuals, as companies, and as institutions.*: Jeff Jarvis, *Public Parts: How Sharing in the Digital Age Improves the Way We Work and Live* (New York: Simon & Schuster, 2015).

Chapter 1 Unleashing the Introvert's Secret Power

11 *The secret to life is to put yourself in the right lighting.*: Susan Cain, *Quiet: The Power of Introverts in a World That Can't Stop Talking* (New York: Broadway Books, 2013).

11 *Carl Jung developed his theory of psychological types*: "Extraversion and introversion," Wikipedia.org, https://en.wikipedia.org/wiki /Extraversion_and_introversion.

11 *"Contrary to popular belief, not all introverts are shy"*: "Introvert" entry, *Urban Dictionary*, https://www.urbandictionary.com /define.php?term=Introvert.

12 *As one scholarly study put it, "An introvert who is silent in a group"*: Aino Sallinen-Kuparinen, James McCroskey, and Virginia P. Richmond, "Willingness to Communicate, Communication, Apprehension, Introversion, and Self-Reported Communication Competence: Finnish and American Comparisons," *Communication Research Reports*, vol. 8, June 1991, pp. 55–64.

14 *For more than twenty years, Judy Wert has led*: See http://www .wertco.com/ and "How the Best Design Recruiter in the Country Finds the Top 1% of Designers," Jared Erondu and Bobby Ghoshal, *TechCrunch*, July 17, 2017, https://techcrunch.com/2017/07/17 /how-the-best-design-recruiter-in-the-country-finds-the-top-1 -of-designers/.

Chapter 2 Why Networking Matters

19 *There is simply too much to be gained from working in tandem with the rest of the world.*: David Benson, "The Power of Asynchronous Communication," *The Social Chic* (blog), April 29, 2012, http:// thesocialchic.com/2012/04/29/the-power-of-asynchronous-com munication/.

19 *Penelope Trunk suggests that staying in one job for three years is a good practice*: "Make Life More Stable by Changing Jobs More Frequently," *Penelope Trunk* (blog), February 25, 2007, http:// blog.penelopetrunk.com/2007/02/25/make-your-life-more-sta ble-by-changing-jobs-more-frequently/.

20 *Hunter Walk . . . describes himself as an introvert*: "How This Anxious Introvert Handles Large Events," Hunter Walk, *Medium*, October 2, 2017, https://medium.com/@hunterwalk/how-this -anxious-introvert-handles-large-events-fc80c7361179.

20 *Similarly, executive recruiter Judy Wert says she gauges her success in being able to connect people*: Interview with the author, February 20, 2018.

21 *"If your network is a mile wide"*: Ivan Misner, "Quantity Is Good, but Quality Is King in Networking," *Business Journals,* June 9, 2017, https://www.bizjournals.com/bizjournals/how-to /marketing/2017/06/in-networking-quantity-is-good-but-quality -is.html.

Chapter 3 The Loose-Touch Habit

31 *Think about how you would approach a potential friend.*: Sourav Dey, "5 Steps to Seriously Improve Your Networking Skills," *Entrepreneur Magazine*, May 14, 2015.

31 *a wry (and not inaccurate) definition*: Herminia Ibarra and Mark Lee Hunter, "How Leaders Create and Use Networks," *Harvard Business Review*, January 2007, https://hbr.org/2007/01/how -leaders-create-and-use-networks.

33 *Non-voice usage . . . surpassed voice calls . . . in 2010*: Jenna Wortham, "Cellphones Now Used More for Data Than for Calls," *New York Times*, May 14, 2010, http://www.nytimes.com/2010/05/14/tech nology/personaltech/14talk.html.

34 *when we let go of communicating only in real time*: David Benson, "The Power of Asynchronous Communication," *The Social Chic* (blog), April 29, 2012, http://thesocialchic.com/2012/04/29 /the-power-of-asynchronous-communication/.

34 *Hyde writes with great insight about what he calls the "gift economy"*: Lewis Hyde, *The Gift: Creativity and the Artist in the Modern World* (New York: Random House, 1979, 2007).

35 *connecting and sharing connections is "kind of like donating money"*: Phone interview with Julie Schlosser, March 1, 2018.

37 *Musician Amanda Palmer has explored*: Amanda Palmer, *The Art of Asking: or How I Learned to Stop Worrying and Let People Help* (New York: Grand Central Publishing, 2014).

41 ¯_(ツ)_/¯ *(a shrug)*: Robinson Meyer, "The Best Way to Type ¯_(ツ)_/¯," *The Atlantic*, May 21, 2014, https://www.the atlantic.com/technology/archive/2014/05/the-best-way-to-type -__/371351/.

41 *sociologist Ray Oldenburg argued for the idea of a "third place"*: "Q+A with Ray Oldenburg," Steelcase Design Q+A, January 8, 2015, https://www.steelcase.com/research/articles/topics/design -q-a/q-ray-oldenburg/.

41 *especially those who are weak ties, are the ones best suited to help you*: David Burkus, *Friend of a Friend: Understanding the Hidden*

Networks That Can Transform Your Life and Your Career (New York: Houghton Mifflin Harcourt, 2018).

44 *Sales pros I know use ticklers*: Interview with Tim Fisher, March 7, 2018.

44 *one of her most fruitful networks*: Interview with Julie Schlosser, March 1, 2018.

Chapter 4 **The Value of Weak Ties**

47 *Weak ties are one of the keys to the future of work*: Jacob Morgan, "Why Every Employee Should Be Building Weak Ties at Work," Forbes.com, March 11, 2014, https://www.forbes.com/sites /jacobmorgan/2014/03/11/every-employee-weak-ties-work/#5d 15cale3168.

47 *"The Strength of Weak Ties," advanced the idea*: M. S. Granovetter, "The Strength of Weak Ties" (1973), *American Journal of Sociology*, 78 (6): 1360–1380, doi:10.1086/225469. The concepts and findings of this work were later published in the monograph *Changing Jobs: Channels of Mobility Information in a Suburban Population*.

49 *"The guy wasn't part of her firm, or even connected"*: Jessi Hempel, "How to Win Founders and Influence Everybody," *Wired*, January 21, 2018, https://www.wired.com/story/margit-wennmach ers-is-andreessen-horowitzs-secret-weapon/.

51 *some of Silicon Valley's global renown "has rested on personal connections"*: Leslie Berlin, *Troublemakers: Silicon Valley's Coming of Age* (New York: Simon & Schuster, 2017).

52 *in a 2015 study of how LinkedIn members found new jobs*: Peter Rigano, "Industries Where Your Network Matters More Than You Think," *LinkedIn* (blog), March 9, 2015, https://blog.linkedin .com/2015/03/09/industries-where-your-network-matters-more -than-you-think.

53 *"The name of the company they work for is, in some ways, an ancillary detail"*: Jeanne G. Harris and Allan A. Alter, "California Dreaming," *Accenture* (blog), date unknown, https://www.accenture

.com/us-en/insight-outlook-california-dreaming-corporate-cul
ture-silicon-valley#block-overview.

54 *Moore's Law means "nothing stays the same for more than a moment"*:
John Markoff, *What the Dormouse Said: How the 60s Counterculture Shaped the Personal Computer Industry* (New York: Viking, 2005), p. xi.

PART TWO   Your Online Toolkit

57 *Humans want and need connection*: Daniel Weitzner, as quoted in Janna Anderson and Lee Rainie, "The Future of Well-Being in a Tech-Saturated World," Pew Research Center for Internet and Technology, April 17, 2018, "The Benefits of Digital Life" section.

Chapter 5   Blending the Personal and Professional

59 *We should see ourselves as a whole and integrated person*: Rebecca Fraser-Thrill, "Forget Work-Life Balance: Aim for Blend Instead," *Huffington Post*, March 27, 2014.

59 *"It's tricky balancing professionalism with personality . . . in addition to showcasing your expertise"*: Cory Fernandez, "This Is What Recruiters Look for on Your Social Media Accounts," *Fast Company*, February 8, 2018, https://www.fastcompany.com/40527752/this-is-what-recruiters-look-for-on-your-social-media-accounts.

60 *I asked Rosemary Fantozzi*: Interview with Rosemary Fantozzi, March 23, 2018.

60 *her professional circle has gravitated*: See, for example, Diego Rodriguez, "Hiring: It's About Cultural Contribution, Not Cultural Fit," LinkedIn Pulse, September 10, 2015, and also Courtney Seiter, "Why We've Stopped Saying 'Culture Fit' and What We're Saying Instead," *Buffer* (blog), April 6, 2017.

60 *Kerry Gallagher made note of the "social media threshold" many people are crossing today*: Kerry Gallagher, "The myth of separate personal and professional social media accounts," *ConnectSafely*

(blog), May 10, 2017, http://www.connectsafely.org/the-myth
-of-separate-personal-and-professional-social-media-accounts/.

62 *"In the old days, we had pretty limited ways to interact with each
other,"*: Interview with Susan Etlinger, March 5, 2018.

63 *Shonda Rhimes tweeted her praise to the judge*: https://twitter.com
/shondarhimes/status/957314856755089410.

63 *a chapter of his favorite new book*: https://www.facebook.com
/BillGates/photos/a.10150331291841961.334784.216311481960
/10155214141051961/?type=3&theater.

63 *Journalist and CNN correspondent Jake Tapper tweets on behalf
of his dog, @winstontapper*: https://twitter.com/WinstonTapper
/status/998905529467580417.

63 *initially said she was stepping down for "personal and family reasons"*: Eileen Daspin, "The Sad and Inspiring Reason This Top
Novartis Exec Stepped Down," *Fortune,* May 31, 2016, http://
fortune.com/2016/05/31/christi-shaw-novartis-resignation/.

63 *"enjoy a perfectly fine mid-life crisis full of bliss and beauty"*: Patrick Pichette, Public retirement announcement, *Google+* (blog),
March 10, 2015, https://plus.google.com/+PatrickPichette
/posts/8Khr5LnKtub.

64 *My former colleague Tim Fisher*: Interview with Tim Fisher, April
2, 2018.

66 *"People do business with people"* . . . *"not faceless, soulless edifices"*: Ann
Handley, "How Do You Balance Your Personal and Professional
Social Media Presence?," annhandley.com, March 2014, updated
March 2018, http://annhandley.com/balance-personal-profes
sional-social-presence/#.WqbNAJPwY3E.

66 *In an interview for this book*: Interview with Ann Handley, March
29, 2018.

68 *Among the 65-plus crowd, 37 percent are social media users*: "Social
Media Fact Sheet," Pew Research Center on Internet and Technology, February 5, 2018, http://www.pewinternet.org/fact-sheet
/social-media/.

Chapter 6　Make Social Media Work for You

71　*While the internet often connects us one-to-one, it also introduces us to new networks*: Sarah Granger, *The Digital Mystique: How the Culture of Connectivity Can Empower Your Life Online and Off* (Berkeley: Seal Press, 2014).

72　*when Facebook opened its service beyond college students*: Interview with Susan Etlinger, March 15, 2018.

74　*"If each of your twenty trusted contacts connected you to twenty more of their own"*: "A Brief History of LinkedIn," https://ourstory .linkedin.com/#year-2003.

75　*Reid Hoffman . . . 2009 interview*: Ellen Lee, "LinkedIn's Startup Story: Connecting the Business World," *CNN Money,* June 2, 2009, http://money.cnn.com/2009/06/02/smallbusiness/linke din_startup_story.smb/.

76　*through LinkedIn Groups meeting people with similar professional interests*: "About LinkedIn," https://about.linkedin.com/7270.

76　*versus just 9 percent of those with a high school diploma or less*: Aaron Smith and Monica Anderson, "Social Media Use in 2018," Pew Research Center for Internet and Technology, March 1, 2018, http://www.pewinternet.org/2018/03/01/social-media -use-in-2018/.

82　*"much relevant experience to display on your Profile"*: Nancy Collamer, "How LinkedIn Groups Can Help You Get a Job," *Next Avenue,* March 5, 2018, https://www.nextavenue.org/linkedin -groups-get-job/.

83　*"just a little bit more reason to say yes"*: Interview with Ryan McDougall, March 9, 2018.

83　*Groups are a place to make contact with context*: Nancy Collamer, "How LinkedIn Groups Can Help You Get a Job," *Next Avenue,* March 5, 2018, https://www.nextavenue.org/linkedin-groups-get -job/.

84　*"insights, opinions, even opportunities, like jobs or gigs"*: Interview with Ryan McDougall, March 9, 2018.

85　*to get you started on what to write about*: Tyrona Heath, "How to Rock Your LinkedIn Profile and Build Your Personal Brand," LinkedIn Pulse, April 3, 2017, https://www.linkedin.com/pulse /how-rock-your-linkedin-profile-build-personal-brand-tyrona-ty -heath/.

88 *Travis Culwell told me an illuminating story*: Email correspondence with Travis Culwell, February 22, 2018. https://docs.google.com /document/d/1K-nDC9-W_xy2L-E9AQfTXow0oNffhNYJ9Ds rWNoVAWI/edit.

89 *"it's the people who are already connected who get all the opportunities"*: Interview with Ryan McDougall, March 9, 2018.

91 *"the tradeoff has been worth it"*: David Carr, "Why Twitter Will Endure," *New York Times,* January 3, 2010, https://www.nytimes .com/2010/01/03/weekinreview/03carr.html.

93 *as digital strategist Erin Blaskie has noted*: "Five Things I Learned About Twitter Bios by Reading over 4,000 User Profiles," *Medium,* July 24, 2017, https://medium.com/@erinblaskie/five-things-i -learned-about-twitter-bios-by-reading-over-4-000-user-profiles -9afe6055c27b.

95 *here are a few ideas about who to follow*: From Hannah Morgan, "10 Ways to Find Relevant People on Twitter," *The Undercover Recruiter,* May 18, 2017, https://theundercoverrecruiter.com /find-follow-twitter/.

95 *typing a hashtag before a keyword or phrase*: Lexi Pandell, "An Oral History of the #Hashtag," *Wired,* May 19, 2017, https://www .wired.com/2017/05/oral-history-hashtag/.

98 *fascinating political treatises*: https://twitter.com/_EthanGrey /status/989375059121901568.

98 *personal stories*: https://twitter.com/michael_nielsen/status /975884635535101952.

98 *asking for a raise*: https://twitter.com/laurahelmuth/status /980579387945967621.

98 *startups in Berlin*: https://twitter.com/I_amGermany/status /976685457378594816.

98 *the tale of an office "lunch thief"*: Cherry Wilson, " 'Stolen Office Lunch' Drama Has Twitter Gripped," BBC News: *Newsbeat,*

March 31, 2018, https://www.bbc.com/news/newsbeat-43 604747.

98 *If you'd like to try tweetstorming*: Nick Douglas, "How to Tweet-storm Without Embarrassing Yourself," *Lifehacker,* June 23, 2017, https://lifehacker.com/how-to-tweetstorm-without-embarrass ing-yourself-1796304750.

100 *800 million users worldwide*: "Who Uses Each Social Media Platform," Pew Research Center for Internet and Technol-ogy, February 5, 2018, http://www.pewinternet.org/fact-sheet /social-media/.

101 *Ryan Cochrane notes, "While someone's Twitter"*: Ryan Cochrane, "The Value of Instagram for Business," LinkedIn Pulse, June 29, 2016, https://www.linkedin.com/pulse/value-instagram-busi ness-ryan-cochrane/.

103 *In an email interview, she told me that Instagram is a key tool*: Email exchange with Alexandra Lange, May 7, 2018.

104 *In an email exchange, he detailed Instagram's crossover value*: Email exchange with Ian Sanders, March 11, 2018.

105 *median number of Facebook friends for US adults*: Aaron Smith, "What People Like and Dislike About Facebook," Pew Research Center, February 3, 2014, http://www.pewresearch.org/fact -tank/2014/02/03/what-people-like-dislike-about-facebook/.

106 *the most useful feature may be Groups*: Christina Newberry, "Every-thing You Need to Know About Using Facebook Groups for Business," *Hootsuite* (blog), December 11, 2017, https://blog .hootsuite.com/facebook-groups-business/.

Chapter 7 **No-Pressure Participation**

109 *The world's collective yearning for connection has . . . created a new status marker*: Nicholas Confessore, Gabriel J. X. Dance, Richard Harris, and Mark Hansen, "The Follower Factory," *New York Times,* January 27, 2018.

110 *across all demographic and age groups*: "Social Media Use over Time," Pew Research Center, February 5, 2018, http://www.pew

internet.org/fact-sheet/social-media; http://www.pewinternet
.org/2018/03/01/social-media-use-in-2018/.

111 *"benevolent lurking"*: Jess Zimmerman, "It's Good to Lurk on
Social Media. At Least for a While," *The Guardian*, June 4, 2015,
https://www.theguardian.com/commentisfree/2015/jun/04/good
-to-lurk-social-media-internet.

113 *social media accounts to screen potential hires*: "Number of Employers
Using Social Media to Screen Candidates at All-Time High, Finds
Latest CareerBuilder Study," *PR Newswire,* June 15, 2017, https://
www.prnewswire.com/news-releases/number-of-employers-using
-social-media-to-screen-candidates-at-all-time-high-finds-latest
-careerbuilder-study-300474228.html.

114 *four distinct strategies for crafting an online persona*: Ariane
Ollier-Malaterre and Nancy P. Rothbard, "How to Separate the
Personal and Professional on Social Media," *Harvard Business
Review*, March 26, 2015, https://hbr.org/2015/03/how-to-sepa
rate-the-personal-and-professional-on-social-media.

117 *Gretchen McCulloch . . . "creative punctuation"*: Gretchen McCulloch, "Will We All Speak Emoji Language in a Couple Years?"
Mental Floss, April 9, 2015, http://mentalfloss.com/article/62584
/will-we-all-speak-emoji-language-couple-years.

117 *"a common crutch to try to express our feelings"*: Lydia Dishman,
"The Business Etiquette Guide to Emojis," *Fast Company,* July
14, 2016, https://www.fastcompany.com/3061807/the-business
-etiquette-guide-to-emojis.

117 *a major* New York Times *feature story called "The Follower Factory"*:
Nicholas Confessore, Gabriel J. X. Dance, Richard Harris, and
Mark Hansen, "The Follower Factory," *New York Times,* January 27, 2018, https://www.nytimes.com/interactive/2018/01/27
/technology/social-media-bots.html.

117 *"the world's collective yearning for connection"*: Confessore et al.,
"The Follower Factory."

118 *"global marketplace for social media fraud"*: Confessore et al., "The
Follower Factory."

119 *"perform for half-assed likes"*: Davida Kugelmass Lederle, "The

Slow Truth to Building an Authentic Brand Online," *The Healthy Maven* (blog), October 25, 2016, https://www.thehealthymaven .com/2016/10/the-slow-truth-to-building-an-authentic-brand -online.html.

119 *"build up their skills"*: Tom Peters, "The Brand Called You," *Fast Company,* August 31, 1997, https://www.fastcompany.com/28905 /brand-called-you.

120 *an authentic online presence*: Mohamed Zohny, "How to Become a Social Media Influencer: The Ultimate Guide," *Medium*, September 20, 2017, https://medium.com/swlh/how-to-become-a -social-media-influencer-the-ultimate-guide-4faddd294bee.

Chapter 8 Email: (Still) the Killer App

123 *Email is actually a tremendous, decentralized, open platform*: Alexis C. Madrigal, "Email Is Still the Best Thing on the Internet," *The Atlantic,* August 14, 2014, https://www.theatlantic.com/technol ogy/archive/2014/08/why-email-will-never-die/375973/.

123 *"cockroach of the Internet"*: Alexis C. Madrigal, "Email Is Still the Best Thing on the Internet," *The Atlantic,* August 14, 2014.

124 *"I try to communicate asynchronously"*: Lance Ulanoff, "Elon Musk: Secrets of a Highly Effective Entrepreneur," *Mashable,* April 13, 2012, http://mashable.com/2012/04/13/elon-musk-secrets-of-ef fectiveness/#dXscKJB.yaqU.

131 *"tend to be more professional"*: Roy Bahat, "Introductions and the 'forward intro email,'" *Also* (blog), October 26, 2016, https:// also.roybahat.com/introductions-and-the-forward-intro-email -14e2827716al.

PART THREE Getting Real

139 *A good improviser is someone who is awake, not entirely self-focused, and moved by a desire to do something useful*: Patricia Ryan Madson, *Improv Wisdom: Don't Prepare, Just Show Up* (New York: Random House, 2005).

Chapter 9 The Real World Beckons

141 *The easiest thing is to react*: Seth Godin, *Tribes: We Need You to Lead Us* (New York: Portfolio Books, 2008).

144 *but remember, it's still work*: Rick Paulas, "When Is a Work Party Really Just Work? Pretty Much Always," *Vice*, April 27, 2018, https://free.vice.com/en_us/article/9kgj7z/work-party-unpaid -labor.

145 *"they're a good excuse"*: Alison Green, as quoted in Paulas, "When Is a Work Party Really Just Work? Pretty Much Always."

147 *"releasing back into the frenzy"*: Hunter Walk, "How This Anxious Introvert Handles Large Events," *Medium*, October 2, 2017, https://hunterwalk.com/2017/10/02/how-this-anxious-introvert -handles-large-events/.

Chapter 10 The Art of Small Talk

155 *When you talk with strangers, you make beautiful and surprising interruptions*: Kio Stark, *When Strangers Meet: How People You Don't Know Can Transform You* (New York: Simon & Schuster/ TED Books, 2017).

156 *"a purely social function"*: Ipek G. Kulahai, Daniel I. Rubenstein, and Asif A. Ghazanfar, "Lemurs Groom-at-a-Distance Through Vocal Networks," *Animal Behaviour,* December 2015, https:// www.princeton.edu/news/2015/12/14/chitchat-and-small-talk -could-serve-evolutionary-need-bond-others.

157 *"no small thing at all"*: Ruth Graham, "In Defense of Small Talk," *Slate,* February 25, 2016, http://www.slate.com/articles/life/cul turebox/2016/02/stop_dismissing_small_talk_as_shallow_or_bor ing_it_s_a_crucial_social_lubricant.html.

Chapter 11 Nuts and Bolts of the Job Hunt

165 *If we wait for the moment when everything, absolutely everything, is ready*: Ivan Turgenev, LibraryofQuotes.com, 2013.

165 *51 percent of Americans holding jobs*: Ed O'Boyle and Annamarie Mann, "American Workplace Changing at a Dizzying Pace," *Gallup News*, February 15, 2017, http://news.gallup.com/busi nessjournal/203957/american-workplace-changing-dizzying-pace .aspx.

167 *lead to an offer*: "Recruiting Funnel Benchmark Report," Jobvite.com, 2017, https://www.jobvite.com/wp-content /uploads/2017/05/Jobvite_2017_Recruiting_Funnel_Bench mark_Report.pdf.

168 *a host of reasons*: Jonathan Blaine, "Busting the '80% of All Jobs Are Hidden' Myth," *Jonathan Blaine* (blog), November 19, 2012, http://jonathanblaine.com/wpress/2012/11/80-percent-of-all-jobs -are-hidden-myth/.

172 *companies with meaningful diversity*: Vivian Hunt, Dennis Layton, and Sara Prince, "Why Diversity Matters," McKinsey & Company, January 2015, https://www.mckinsey.com/business-func tions/organization/our-insights/why-diversity-matters.

Chapter 12 **You've Got This**

177 *Liberation does not come from outside*: Gloria Steinem, "Interview with Gloria Steinem," CBS News, December 20, 1999, https:// www.cbsnews.com/news/interview-with-gloria-steinem/.

179 *In a 2014 report,* The Atlantic *cited a study*: Katty Kay and Claire Shipman, "The Confidence Gap," *The Atlantic,* May 2014, https:// www.theatlantic.com/magazine/archive/2014/05/the-confidence -gap/359815/.

181 *Human resources journalist Tony Lee reminds new grads*: Tony Lee, "Networking After College," CareerCast.com, June 2010, updated January 7, 2017, https://www.careercast.com/career-news /networking-after-college.

181 *A 2018 study from job search service CareerBuilder*: Press release, "More Than Half of Workers 60+ Are Postponing Retirement," CareerBuilder, April 26, 2018, http://press.careerbuilder.com/2018

-04-26-More-than-Half-of-Workers-60-are-Postponing-Retire
ment-According-to-New-CareerBuilder-Study.

185 *"getting into tech"*: Karen Wickre, "How to 'Get into Tech' If
You're Not an Obvious Fit," *Wired*, February 27, 2015, https://
www.wired.com/2015/02/how-to-get-into-tech-if-youre-not-an
-obvious-fit/.

186 *you can position yourself as a "men-tern"*: Bill Tobin, "Be a Men-
tern: Both a Mentor & Intern at the Same Time . . ." *Medium*,
February 27, 2017, https://medium.com/@CultureDev/be-a-men
-tern-both-a-mentor-intern-at-the-same-time-c6c41d64bcd9.

186 *the seasoned hotelier and entrepreneur*: Chip Conley, *Wisdom @
Work: The Making of the Modern Elder* (New York: Crown Books,
2018).

188 *Sree took his job search public*: His story was featured in several
places, including Jenni Avins, "The Met Ousted a Top Executive,
So He Used Facebook to Show the World How to Do Unem-
ployment Right," *Quartz*, June 23, 2016, https://qz.com/711943
/sree-sreenivasan-how-to-spin-getting-fired-from-your-high-pro
file-job-into-a-delightful-digital-campaign/; and a feature on *PBS
NewsHour*, Roben Farzad, "How One Digital Expert Turned His
Social Network into a New Job," August 4, 2016, https://www
.pbs.org/newshour/economy/social-network-new-job.

189 *John Wooden famously lived by a seven-point creed*: "Coach John
Wooden's 7-Point Creed," news release, UCLA, June 4, 2010,
http://newsroom.ucla.edu/releases/xx-wooden-seven-point-creed
-84181.

Afterword

191 *As Stanford business professor Chip Heath put it*: As quoted in Nina
Martin, "The Reinvention Chronicles," *San Francisco Magazine*,
May 24, 2010, https://www.modernluxury.com/san-francisco
/story/the-reinvention-chronicles.

Index

About the Author

Karen Wickre is the former editorial director for Twitter. She held a similar role at Google for nearly a decade and has worked in Silicon Valley for thirty years. She has been a columnist for Wired .com and serves on several boards, including the John S. Knight Journalism Fellowship program at Stanford, the International Center for Journalists, and the News Literacy Project. She is also a cofounder of Newsgeist, an annual unconference fostering new approaches to news. She lives in San Francisco.